Java™ for Kids

(and grown-ups)
Nadia Ameziane Garcia

Cover design: Pixel Dizajn Studio
Illustrations from Pixabay.com under CC0 license.

2nd Edition, March 2018

www.icodeyoutoo.com

Java™ for Kids

(and grown-ups)

Nadia Ameziane Garcia

Introduction (for parents and teachers)

First of all, <u>thank you very much</u> for bothering on leafing through this book. For wanting to familiarize yourself -and to know firsthand- the waters your daughter, pupil or whatever relationship ties you, is going to dive into.

Maybe you have some previous coding skills -maybe you are a real eminence! - and you are just looking for ideas to present these skills in a creative or playful way. If that's the case you'll notice that some topics are just briefly explained in this book. That's because I've tried to put general ideas ahead of details, to acquaint the learner with the way he must express instructions rather than with the thousand details or possibilities every instruction may hide.

If, on the contrary, you haven't had any prior contact with this discipline, don't be afraid. I didn't write this book to leave no one behind, and if you follow through you'll see the concepts are clear and succinct, so I am sure you will be able to lend a hand if asked to. Besides, after the introduction you'll find a guide with everything you need to prepare in your computer. I won't let you look bad 😉

And maybe you are an unabashed adult who bought this book for him or herself; if that is the case **congratulations for you too**! I am convinced I can teach you a couple things. Although I thought of this book as a guide to teach little humans from 8 to 18 years old, everything you are going to read will suit you too.

A couple more things you might be wondering

Maybe you are wondering **what can coding do for your child.** Truth is, I'm still wondering what it is that it can NOT do.

Coding is an excellent way of building new bridges in our way of thinking: it predisposes us to approach the questions presented before our eyes in a **LOGICAL** manner. It makes us get used to **SET IN ORDER** the available data, to approach any problem more efficiently. I always say that, inside the mind of every person that learns how to program, to express himself through algorithms, some kind of *click* occurs -and it has no turning back. The *programmer's mindset* becomes a tool you will always keep, and it will be useful in so many aspects of life.

By coding you also test your **PATIENCE and FRUSTRATION TOLERANCE.** Sometimes a piece of code is a chess game against ourselves. Suddenly something just won't work out, and although we don't know why, we just can't leave it half done. When this happens, we keep on programming inside our heads while we are on our way to school, taking a shower or going for a walk... until, on the spur of the moment, the solution of the puzzle lights up our mind: *eureka!* **The feeling of having overcome that step -of having grown a little more- every time this happens is an immense gift for anyone, but even more for a developing person.**

Learning to program has a social dimension too... wipe all your prejudices out of your mind, delete all the images of 200-pounds boys who live on soda and can't be away from their computers. Both online as in person, coding makes us share, contrast, collaborate... coding urges us to team up, share our projects and knowledge, makes us look at other people's code and learn from their failures and success. To gather with other hectic little brains.

Last but not least, **programming is DEMOCRATIC.** You don't need any special abilities, it is not limited to a certain age range nor is it limited by any disability. You won't need expensive gear or proprietary software. Anyone can learn anytime.

You may be wondering if coding is fitting for your kid, who seems to be an arts oriented person. Although it may seem like some kind of black magic, only intended for brainy people, I can tell that coding is not specifically related to science learning. It is a multidisciplinary activity that transcends all the divisions our educative system insists on setting. It's a very powerful tool that can serve the artistic and creative mind, as well as it can satisfy scientific concerns. And, to be honest, **sometimes the best programs are born of our laziness.** From the desire to automate boring tasks that we don't want to do -or that we want to reduce to a couple seconds- big occasions are born, to think, to engineer and to work on our abstract thinking, a mandatory tool for every student.

Finally, about the **learning objectives for this book.**
Well, my idea was not to turn the kid or teen into an expert programmer: this book does not replace the formal studies in this area. My romantic pursue was to spark their curiosity. **Drawing a path as easy to follow as it can be, without great amounts of theory and fussy conditions, so the reader can build his very own scripts all by himself and from the very start of their journey.**

My goal is to make the apprentice feel challenged, involved and able. Make him own the basic skills so he can build anything his mind imagines, so he never does things just because, without understanding why does it work. I believe that their own need to go further will drive them into broadening those skills I am about to just outline for them, and nothing can make me happier than knowing that my reader ends this book longing for more. Because if there is any universal truth in this world in the art of coding, it's that one never finishes learning.

Introduction (for trainees)

¡Congrats! You are almost a programmer. Thank you for trusting me for such a mission.

In this book, I wanted to unveil a secret that any other textbooks seem to try to hide: coding is funny. I like it because it is one of the few ways in this world to make dreams come true (okay, *certain* dreams). It's true that coding is not an infallible system, but personally I don't know of many other ways to make an idea become a command, and to make this command be obeyed making REAL what once only existed inside my brain.

Furthermore, for us nosy people programming is a chance to try figuring out how some of our everyday objects work, objects that maybe didn't catch our attention until today. The minute you learn a couple thinks you start seeing the world through new glasses, imagining what's cooking inside your favorite video game, that vending machine or even inside a supermarket scale. You wonder if the instructions that make them possible are the same you would write. Maybe even -if you are like me- you love going a little farther: you wonder if they have considered every possible way of using that appliance. You wonder if you can find that unforeseen combination of user actions that can make it crash.

Anyway, I've tried to pen an entertaining and interesting book. I want you to be able to produce little programs as soon as possible, applying any new detail you learn. I have not included anything rather than the basics, so my advice for you is simple: **don't run, don't skip chapters** and follow their order.

¡Oh! Every now and then you'll see some **annotations inside grey boxes.** Those are little clues I've left for you, just in case you want to investigate some topics a little more. You can also leave those boxes aside and go back to them when you finish the book, and of course you can also ignore them forever: you are the boss here!

Just two more tips:

If you like this, be patient. Don't be too demanding with your poor self: you live and learn! Give yourself every chance you need.

If you don't like this, leave this book aside, no regrets! Even for the youngest people, life is too short to go chasing trains one doesn't want to take.

Enjoy the ride!

INDEX

¿What will I need?

In order to see through the hands-on exercises I will come up with, you will need a computer. You can work with a Linux-based operative system such as Ubuntu (and that would be fantastic!) or with any flavor of Windows or MacOS.

A working internet connection will also be useful 😊

Software and components you will need

JDK, or Java™ Development Kit. To be able to run our creations you need your machine to read into the Java code.
You can download it for free at Oracle.com, on their Downloads section. Remember to look for the Java SE Development Kit 8, as this book is based on that specific version.

Remember to **verify that you are getting the right package for your OS (Windows, Mac…) and processor type (X86 or X64)**. If you don't know what kind of processor you are working with, you can check it on your machine, inside the machine info section (it will be named System, MyPC, About this Mac or something similar).

Once you have the JDK you'll have to set your **environment variable**. This process is different for every operative system, but very simple anyway. I suggest you let yourself be guided by the steps you'll find on Oracle's site: *https://www.java.com/es/download/help/path.xml*

Text editor. To work on the practices, it would be great for you to stick to a text editor as simple as possible. Some powerful and free editors are Notepad++, Atom and Vim. I'll use the first one for my examples.

You can download Notepad++ at *https://notepad-plus-plus.org/*

Command prompt. If you work with Windows you can use its native Command Prompt app. If you work with Ubuntu or Mac you can use the Terminal app. I strongly recommend you make yourself familiar with the commands needed to browse through folders, open files and so on. A quick search on the Wikipedia will show you a list of the commands you will need.

You won't need and IDE (integrated development environment) or any special software. Every activity in this book has been designed so that you can complete it with just a text processor.

0. That black magic called *coding...*

I am afraid that, prior to putting ourselves to work, there's a couple things you must know about your machine and the way it works. **Programming is like *talking to the computer*, and if we don't know the way it thinks we'll have a hard time making it listen to us.**

Like you may already know, a program is **a script made of orders that your computer follows to perform a series of operations.** Problem here is, that computer doesn't speak our language, but one we call "machine code" and that, to make it even more complicated, that language is different for every type of processor. This machine code is made of numbers that account for different types of operations, values and other data and that list every single action.

Writing machine code ourselves would be terribly slow and complex, and that's why there are other languages designed to be used by us people -such as Java, the one we'll learn with this book. When we run the program, these languages are translated to another one your machine can understand. So, even though a little piece of Java code may seem confusing to you, the truth is that is just an *easily readable, human-friendly* piece of code that needs proper translating to machine-friendly code. That translation is performed by a program we call *compiler or interpreter*.

When we **compile** the code we've written, the compiler reads our instructions, verifies we have written them correctly -even when they might be *the wrong instructions*- and, if that's the case, it translates them to machine readable code. If we wrote them wrong then it won't compile them: instead it will warn us of our mistake. Don't take it too personally, even the most expert programmers deal with this daily.

Writing magic: algorithms

Now we already know that when we code we do it in a language designed for us humans to feel more comfortable, and that we have it translated afterwards so that our processor can understand it.

But, how do we organize those sets of orders?
Our machine is completely literal: it won't perform anything we don't command, and it will do everything we ask him to. It will always have that need for us to specify what, how and when, and even what to if something goes wrong.

To express those orders in an organized and neat manner we must have a method, a discipline in the way we detail our commands. That is where algorithms come to play. Wikipedia says - and I won't be the one to disagree- that **an algorithm is a set of rules that precisely defines a sequence of operations**. We can picture it as the sequence of instructions we would give someone who has to do something specific and has no idea of how to do it.

An example of an algorithm we could write for someone who doesn't know how to water a plant:

1. Grab the watering can

2. Place it under the faucet
3. Turn the faucet's handle until water starts coming out of it
4. Keep it open until there are 16oz of water inside the can
5. Turn the faucet's handle to the opposite side, until water stops flowing
6. Carry the watering can to the garden
7. Locate the plant you need to water
8. Tilt the watering can above the plant until water stars flowing; keep it tilted while there is water in it
9. Put the water can back in its place

As you can see there are several important details we must specify to help our gardener apprentice:

- The *order* of the actions to perform
- *When* does every action *end*
- *What to do afterwards*

If we don't provide him with the correct order, he may end up watering first and filling the can afterwards… and making the plant athirst! If we don't tell him when to close the faucet, our friend might flood the house. And if we don't advise him to put the can back in its place after pouring the water, he might well remain with the can tilted on its hand forever. That's how literal our friend is, just like a computer… and that is why **algorithms must be exact, have a specific order and an ending.**

And this is all the previous theory you needed to learn before starting to type. **Hooray!**

EXERCISES

Now I suggest you do some easy exercises, just to make sure you didn't get something wrong. We don't want to kill our plants, do we? ☺
(you'll find the solutions on page 20, but don't look at them before completing the tasks!)

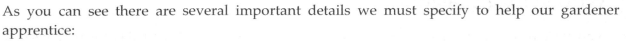

1.   The processor can execute your Java code

a)   Of course it can

b)   No way!

2.   An algorithm is…

a)   A code designed so the computer understands it

b)   A sequence of exact commands with an order and an ending

3.   To understand the language you're coding in, your computer needs translations...

a)   Performed by a processor

b)   Performed by an interpreter

AVOIDING DISASTER

This algorithm has some mistakes in it… they could lead us to disaster! Can you spot them and correct it?

How to cook fries:

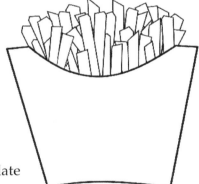

1. Peel all the potatoes you want to cook
2. Grab a peeling knife
3. Start peeling the potatoes
4. Put the frying pan on the stove
5. Light the stove and set it to medium heat
6. Pour oil in the pan
7. Throw the peeled potatoes inside the pan
8. Fry the potatoes
9. Take the fries out of the pan and put them in a plate

Extra practices, for dedicated students… 😊

Write your own algorithm

Create a sequence of instructions for an imaginary task. I suggest some ideas:
- Ironing a shirt
- Sending a letter
- Cleaning your teeth
- Doing a side braid on your own hair

- Tying your shoes
- Blowing up a balloon

SOLUTIONS

Quiz solutions:
1 - b
2 - b
3 - b

Algorithm mistakes:
Instructions to cook fries
1. Peel all the potatoes you want to cook
2. Grab a peeling knife
3. Start peeling the potatoes *until all of them are peeled*
4. *Slice* the peeled potatoes *(you don't want to fry whole potatoes!)*
5. Put the frying pan on the stove
6. Light the stove and set it to medium heat
7. Pour *half a cup* of oil in the pan *(we don't want to be left forever with the oil bottle in our hand or overflow the pan...)*
8. *When the oil is hot* Throw the peeled potatoes inside the pan
9. Fry the potatoes *until they are golden brown/for x minutes*
10. Take the fries out of the pan and put them in a plate
11. *Turn of the stove (so you don't end up burning the house)*

As you can see, this is a simulation and not a real program (although we might as well be coding the software for a cooking robot). The purpose of this exercise was to notice how important it is to specify what instructions to perform, in which order, and when to stop performing them so we don't get stuck in an infinite loop (this is something you'll understand later in this book).

1. The book of spells

Now we already know that **we code in a special language, designed for humans,** and that we use that language to write algorithms, which are sequences of operations we need the processor to perform.

But **how what does that process look like when we speak about a real program?** In this chapter, we will finally see that, and when you reach to the end of it you will write your very own program.

As we said before, this book is based in Java language for learning. And when you want to execute a Java program in your computer you need three ingredients:

- **A text editor** to write your code. You don't need anything special, a free one will do.
- **A java compiler,** to produce what we call *bytecode.*
- **The interpreter** that will make it possible for your computer to understand what you wrote in your code

According to the level of knowledge you will reach in this chapter, a Java program is just a bunch of code written with the text editor and saved as a .java file -so or computer knows that it must read its content as Java code.

Camel humps

There are some rules to name our code files in the programming world. In the particular case of the Java language, this rule is known as *UpperCamelCase* (because the shape of the word resembles a camel's back and their famous humps) to help us remind that when we name a java code file we must join every word in that name together and capitalize the first letter of every word.

This is a good way to ease our computer's job and avoid errors... and, look closely: names written by that rule really resemble a camel's back!

A couple examples of correct filenames:
```
MyFirstProgram.java
RuleTheWorld.java
```

And a couple filenames that BREAK that rule could be:
```
rebelProgram.java
mariascode.java
```
Naming our files like that won't produce an error *per se,* but following the rules will give our work consistency and save ourselves future headaches.

But let's go to the heart of the matter. How can be write valid commands? Should I just write whatever and pray to be understood? Is it enough if I write in English?

Well, not at all. As in any good magic, **coding is based in libraries and books full of spells that someone wrote way before us... once we apply them properly upon an object we cast a specific spell.**

When we downloaded the JDK we also grabbed all that bunch of libraries and spells that compose the Java language, and when we write our program we will invoke them according to the language rules. One of that rules, lest not forget it, is that **we'll refer to the spells as methods and talk about these books as classes.**

Once we start coding (and that will happen in only a couple more pages, I promise) what we're going to do is calling the classes we want to use, so that they listen to us and then allow us the use of their methods.

Hello, World!

"Hello, World" are traditionally the first two words everyone writes upon making their debut as programmers, and we are going to follow that tradition.

Let's move on to the code. Here you have a code example, the first we will analyze and understand.

```
HelloWorld.java
1    public class HelloWorld {
2
3    public static void main (String[] args) {
4
5        //show text on screen
6
7        System.out.println("Hello, World");
8        }
9
10   }
```

→ **Pay attention: this font will appear every time I want you to notice that the text is Java code**

First thing we can read in this piece of code is **"public class"**. We write this at the beginning of the document, thus when the compiler reaches that point it will know that from there on everything it is going to find is a Java class. Incidentally, upon doing this we are naming our class -and as you can see the name is *HelloWorld*.

The next thing we read is **"public static void main..."** this sentence we will write **always** as a header for our most important class -which we know as *the main class*. Think of it like some kind of password that opens our spell.

That "abracadabra public static void blahblahblah"

This apparently nonsense, weird verbiage we have written appears always in the main class of the program and, even though you don't need to worry about this for now, maybe you'll appreciate knowing what the heck does it mean.
Our class is:

Public, because sometimes you will write secret methods that other parts of the program can't see. But as we said before this is the main class, the entrance of our program, and we want the compiler to be able to access it… and so we set it as public.

Static, because we don't want to turn our class into an object. I know you don't understand this by now, it's magic for *connoisseurs.*

Void, because some methods have the power of returning us something after we cast our spell. And when they can't, we must state it calling them *void* to prevent the system to remain waiting endlessly for that return.

Main, because that is what this class is. By setting it as *main* we are announcing that this is where the core of our application resides. This is the start line.

String args is a part of the spell that allows us to execute the program with special orders. Don't think about it, you won't get to use that possibility in this book. But it's ok to just know *why* we do things instead of repeating them just because 😊

After that we have **an annotation that starts with a double slash (//).** We call that *commenting.* Those slashes are an *invisibility spell*! If you put them before a sentence your app will run without noticing them, which is very useful. You can use comments to write things you want to remember later, such as reminders of what a specific piece of code was written for, without *bothering* the compiler.
And there's even more: for a single line of code you can write the two slashes, but if you want to comment a whole paragraph you can use an **invisibility shield, /*like that*/,** and the program will just run without *seeing* that paragraph.

```
//this is a single line comment
```

```
/*and this would be
a whole paragraph
of commented text
ignored just by being inside this shield*/
```

Finally, we have the *spell* we cast. We have used a spell known as println, it has the ability of making your computer write things on the terminal screen. But not anything: it will write whatever you put inside the parentheses, between quotation marks (that's what we call the *parameter*).

We write the method with the following structure:

```
method ("parameter text") ;
```

Namely, always:
- the method first,
- and after that, in a cloud of smoke… (okay, inside a parentheses and quotation marks) the text we want to put a spell on, so it appears on the screen

And now look at the program again: it seems easier, doesn't it? Everything makes sense now: I open the book (the class), announce I am about to make some magic (main method) and then I can start casting spells (my System.out.println method).

```
public class HelloWorld {

    public static void main(String[] args) {
        // Show my text on the screen
        System.out.println("Hello, World");
    }
}
```

{ And just to make clear that **every piece of code is contained inside the other,** we put them into this brackets {}.

Don't forget to put them or the compiler will complain, as it won't find your class and methods' start and ending. }

Our first practice

We are going to write our very first program.
Follow the steps carefully:

1. Launch your text editor and copy the program we just analyzed. I suggest you write it down yourself from your memory instead of just copying from the example. Later on you can compare and see if you forgot anything.
2. Save the file. **Don't forget to name it just like the class -and according to the Upper-CamelCase rule.** Set the file extension as *.java.*
3. Now we are going to *compile* the program. From the terminal, and located inside the file's folder (if you don't know how to do this, go back to the *What we are going to need* chapter) write the command *javac* followed by a blank space and the name of the file you have saved, including its extension:
   ```
   javac HelloWorld.java
   ```
   The compiler will then create a new file inside the same folder, called HelloWorld.class, and that's the one we will run. Notice that if everything has gone ok with the compiler, it won't show you any message.
4. Run your app! To do this, just write *java* in the terminal followed by a blank space and the name of the program -no extensions here or you will get an error!
   ```
   java HelloWorld
   ```

¡**Eureka!** Our program runs and thanks to our magic spell the terminal window shows our first message to the world.

Something went wrong? If some error appeared when you tried to compile your program, check for the following
   - Class and file names must be the same
   - Your code looks like the one in my example
   - You wrote the correct extension when naming your file

Don't worry if it doesn't work on your first try... with a Little love and serenity, and following every instruction, step by step, it will eventually work out.

ACTIVITIES

Based on the program we just created, try to code the following modifications:

- A program that instead of "Hello, World" says "Bye, bye, crocodile"
- A program that says "Hello World" and after that "The weather's good today"

MAKE SOME EXPERIMENTS:

- Including more than one message -each one between its quoation marks- inside the same parentheses
- Adding or deleting curly braces ({})
- Adding or deleting semicolons ";"
- Changing the program name -the one stated in the main class- to make it different with the file name.

Try to compile and run the app after each change. What happens when you make these changes? What messages do you receive from the compiler? Is it possible to run your app like that?

SOLUTIONS

- To modify the text that is shown on the screen you just have to change what you wrote in the println method, between quotation marks -don't forget them. That is, to change the parameter you pass to the method.
- To write two messages, you can repeat the method:
  ```
  System.out.println("Hello, World");
  System.out.println("The weather's good today");
  ```
  Or put the two messages inside the same method, separated by a comma
  ```
  System.out.println("Hello, World", "The weather's good today");
  ```
  Although that won't look as nice as the first solution, because they will appear one right next to the other.

There are, of course, other ways to do that, but you will learn about that later.

For now, with these activities you learned that you can write all the methods you need inside the same class, inside the curly braces of the main method; and even passing more than one parameter (messages between quotation marks) to the println method.

2. A variable treasure

Now that we already know a couple things about how a program is set and the proper way of casting spells, it is time to know a new, super important device: **variables**.

In this chapter we will learn **what are they, how many types are there and how to start managing them** with our apps.

¿What are variables in programming?

Coding manuals tells us that **a variable is a memory space in your computer, where you store a value that you assigned to it.** There are different types of variables, according to the type of information you want to keep inside them.

But this sounds a tad dense, so in this chapter -to better understand that definition- we will instead work with a treasure we created magically. Because we are magicians, aren't we?

Our treasure is stored in an enormous arch, which will act as our computer's memory. That arch guards a lot of very valuable data -all kinds and shapes of data!
In our inventory we have several types of elements, that we use to the occasion. The most common are:

char – chars are little gems. When they are backlit you can see each one of them hides **a character inside** (a sign, number or letter) guarded by single quotes.

int – Ints are golden coins, each one with **a particular numeric value** which can range from a very, very low value way under zero until… well, a gigantic number, very difficult to picture.

double/ float – coins always store integers -that is, numbers without fractional components- so there are times when we need to write a cheque to pay numeric values that contain commas, such as 25,75$. Doubles and floats are exactly that: **comma separated numeric values**.

strings- Strings are necklaces we use to form linked series of ordered chars, fastened with double quotation marks. We can **store series of ordered chars** we don't want to mess, in string variables. It would be sad if they ended up scattered all around the arch!

bool – booleans are not treasures themselves, but they help us guarding them. They are **little padlocks with just two possible values: true or false** (open or close). You may be wondering what use can they be, and you will discover it in the future.

Now let's go back the matter. What does **variable** mean? A variable is **a unique space located inside our arch, with a specific name, that matches one of the types we have just seen and has a concrete value.** Some examples of variables inside our treasure chest could be the following:

- A char called *initial*, with the value 'i'
- An int called salary, with value 1500
- A double, or a float, named *price*, with value 1,45
- A string called *salute*, with value "Hello"
- A boolean called *open* with value "true"

When we write our programs, **we can create as many variables as we need.** We can create them (or *declare* them, like experts say) at the very start of the program to have them generated when it starts running, or inside the methods, so they appear when they are executed.

You will see there are a ton of operations we can do with our variables, even with little programming knowledge.

We can perform math operations with ints and doubles. We can trim, reorder or truncate strings. We can teach the app how to make its decisions using booleans... your imagination is the only limit.

The proper way of creating a variable is with the *type – name – value* schema. Thus we declare AND initialize the variables we wrote before:

```
char initial = 'i';
int salary = 1500;
float price = 1.45;
String salute = "Hello";
bool open = true;
```

→ **Pay attention!** We write the char's values between single quotes and the string's values between double quotation marks.

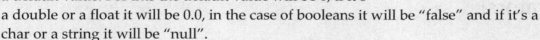

A simple activity: printing variables

Let's start from our Hello World program again. This time, instead of writing the text to show on screen *inside* the method, we will just pass a variable to that method and it will show its value on the screen.

Copy this program, compile it and make it run:

```
1   public class HelloWorld {
2
3   public static void main (String[] args) {
4       char a = "u";
5       int price = 100;
6       String salute = "Hello, World";
7
8       //show text on screen
9
10      System.out.println(u);
11      System.out.println(100);
12      System.out.println(salute);
13
14      System.out.println(price*2);
15      }
16
17   }
```

31

Look at it. We declared and initialized our variables at the beginning, so we can simply pass them to the println method and it will print (show onscreen) their value.

But, what happened on line 14? Look closely at the outcome of your program… it multiplied the value of *price* by the number we wrote in the method and just printed the result. Why did the program behave like that?

¡Operators!

¡Congratulations! You just discovered the **operators: magic symbols that perform operations on our variables.**

There are many types of operators. Some of the most commonly used are arithmetic operators, which you can use to manipulate numerical variables (int, float, double…): +, -, *, /… and that basically perform math operations. Generally, **you can't use arithmetic operators on non-numeric variables** (except for the + symbol, which can be used for string concatenation).

It's easy to work with these magical symbols, you just have to know the purpose of each one of them. I have set up a guide for you, so you can come back to it every time you need to use them. You don't need to memorize this table, we are not here to repeat things just because… ☺ Practice makes perfect and in you will eventually start to remember them without checking the guide.

=	Simple assignment operator

Arithmetic Operators

+	Additive operator / String concatenation
-	Subtraction
*	Multiplication
/	Division
%	Finds the remainder in a division. I.e., 7 % 5 = 2

Unary operators

+	Positive values
-	Minus: negative values
++	Increments a value by 1
--	Decrements a value by 1
!	Inverts the value of a Boolean

Equality and relational operators

==	Equal to
!=	Not equal to
>	Greater than
>=	Greater than or equal to
<	Less than
<=	Less than or equal to

Conditional operators

&&	Conditional-AND: "Monday && Friday" means "both"
||	Conditional-OR: "Monday || Friday" means "one of these two"
?:	Ternary. You won't use it in this book 😊

Type comparison operator

instanceof	Compares an object to a type. I.e. "5.6 instanceof Double" = true

Let's have a look at a couple examples of operators' usage. Do you dare guessing what will these programs show on the screen?

```
1   public class FamilyAge{
2
3   public static void main (String[] args){
4
5       int dadAge = 46;
6       int momAge = 47;
7
8       //show text on screen
9
10      System.out.println("Dad's age is: " + dadAge);
11      System.out.println("Mom's age is: " + momAge);
12
13      int ageAddition = dadAge + momAge;
14
15      System.out.println("Their ages add up to: " + ageAddition + " years.");
16
17      }
18  }
```

```
1   public class FamilyAge{
2
3   public static void main (String[] args){
4
5       int dadAge = 46;
6       int momAge = 47;
7       int sonAge = 10;
8
9       String resultMessage = "Their ages add up to ");
10
11      //show text on screen
12
13      System.out.println("Dad's age is: " + dadAge);
14      System.out.println("Mom's age is: " + momAge);
15      System.out.println("Mom is " + (momAge - dadAge) + " year older than Dad.");
16
17      }
18  }
```

If you compile and run them you will see that with the + and – operators you can perform arithmetic operations or link texts.

Furthermore, we can use operators to change the value of a variable, as we did in the example below when initializing the variable ageAdittion.
We initialized it as the result of an addition, but we could have performed any other operation.
For example, here we are initializing a new variable, stating that its value will be the result of a division between other two:

34

```
int agesResult = momAge / dadAge;
```

or we could have used an equality operator:

```
int momAge = dadAge;
```

meaning that momAge will be created with the same value that dadAge has in that specific moment.

(In case you may be wondering, even if dadAge changes its value later, momAge won't. That's because they are separate and totally different memory locations and what happens later to one of them won't affect the other. You know, if I take a selfie today and cut my hair tomorrow, my selfie won't change with me: my selfie just reflects my looks on a specific moment in time).

All this adding up, decrementing and equaling variables... it can be done because they all belong to the same data type. If you try to write:

```
String a = dadAge;
```

You'll get a compiler error, because you can't give a string the value you had stored in an int. You know they are not the same kind of jewel, and therefore they just won't fit.

¡Camel attack!

Do you remember that *UpperCamelCase* rule? That obligation to name our program with concatenated words and capitalizing the first letter of each one of them.

When we name variables, we follow another rule called *LowerCamelCase*, and so we must name it like that: concatenated words, capitalize each first letter EXCEPT FOR THE FIRST WORD which will remain low case.

```
int age;
float minimumHeight;
double averageWomenWeight;
```

Yes, the compiler will understand us even if we don't follow it, but anyway it's a good practice and it will help us in the future, when we get to share our work with fellow programmers.

Some challenges using variables and operators

Let's dare to face some advanced challenges. To do that, we will use new methods we still haven't heard of.

We'll get to know **the Scanner class** (remember: a class is like a book that contains spells related to the same topic), and the Scanner class contains -no surprise here- the Scanner method. This powerful method gives us the opportunity to **talk to the program through the keyboard**, while the app is running.

If we want to use that class first we've got to make it available to our program. And we do that by adding this command at the beginning of the class:

```
import java.util.Scanner;
```

Little boxes

Although we cannot see it, **classes belong to packages.**

Sometimes instead of importing a single class, what we do is importing the whole container package, which includes the desired class as well as other classes we may need.

Once we have imported the class, we are ready to summon its methods. Picture it as if we had grabbed the book from the library to start reading spells from it.

To use the Scanner we follow these steps:

- **We open a new Scanner**, and name it as we wish:
  ```
  Scanner janeDoe = new Scanner(System.in);
  ```
  (Pay attention: a new Scanner, called janeDoe, that reads from System.in -or, for that matter, the user's keyboard. Notice how the keyboard is expressed between parentheses, because it's a parameter for the reader method).

- **We create a variable of the desired type.** And when initializing it, we set its value as "whatever the user writes in the keyboard". Just like that:
  ```
  int i = janeDoe.nextInt();
  ```

(And because we created it as an int type, the program will expect a number with no commas. Notice how we have used the method in the same way we learnt before when we started using println: *method name-dot-parameter*. Or, in this case, *janeDoe-dot-next Int that comes through the keyboard*).

Now everything's set for us to write. The app will catch what we write and store it in the memory chest, as the value of one of our jewels -a variable.

Other ways of invoking the Scanner

We have learnt one way to invoke the Scanner
so it can read numbers and store them as int variables. **If we
want to read any other type of data we just must declare the right type of variable.**
Supposed we keep on working with that Scanner called janeDoe. For example, let's
make it read strings:

```
String myString = janeDoe.nextLine();
```

Or booleans:

```
bool myBoolean = janeDoe.nextBoolean();
```

And so on, to read floats, chars…
But, what shall I do if I don't know what kind of data will I receive from the user?
Well, to sort that you'll need decision making statements. You'll learn that in the
next lesson 😌

Electronic piggy bank

Let's design a program that serves us as piggy bank. The app will have the features listed below:
- Accept money
- Count money
- Show your balance

1. Write the algorithm that describes the process of using the piggy bank. There is not a unique correct answer, just try to be as specific as possible.

2. Match the following items to the method or tool you could use for them:

ACCEPT MONEY	SHOW BALANCE	COUNT MONEY	INSERT VALUE

System.out.println	Scanner	User's keyboard	Arithmetic operators

3. Once solved, **the activity above gives you a hint on the way this app's code could look like.**

Try to write the code, it's ok if it doesn't compile. This is an engineering challenge!
After that, check my suggested solution (remember, there isn't a unique solution) and make the changes you need so your code works.

4. Play with your new app. Try to make it crash. Try to enter negative values… what happens if you do that?

Optional activity: only for advanced pupils

Are you capable of modifying the program so it's able to accept doubles and floats? By doing that your piggy bank would allow storage of *check*s as well.
Can you change the code so the bank accepts Strings too? It would be nice to have a place for *necklaces* in the bank too.
TIP: go back to "other ways of invocating the Scanner", maybe there you will find what you need.

SOLUTIONS

1. **Algorithm.**

> This is not a single answer question, but here you are my suggestion:

- Program starts running
- Balance is shown on screen
- The program asks the user for the amount to deposit
- The user enters the value
- The value is added to the initial balance
- New updated balance is shown on the screen

2. Accept money - Scanner
   Show balance - System.out.println
   Count money – Arithmetic operators
   Insert value – User keyboard

3. In order to **arrange your piggy bank so it can accept necklaces or checks**, you just have to create variables that suit these datatypes and use the same scanner as many times as needed. Try with this piece of code. (please note: you can set any initial balance):

```java
1  import java.util.Scanner;
2
3  public class myScanner{
4
5      public static void main(String []args){
6
7          int balance = 0;
8          String neckLaces = null;
9
10         System.out.println("Your balance is " + balance);
11
12         //ask the user
13         System.out.println("Please enter the amount to deposit");
14
15         //summon the scanner
16         Scanner myScanner = new Scanner(System.in);
17
18         //create a variable to store the deposit
19         String myDeposit = myScanner.nextLine();
20         neckLaces = myDeposit;
21
22         //show current balance
23         System.out.println("Your balance is " + balance + ". Your necklace balance is "
           + necklaces +". Thanks for making a deposit.");
24
25
26  }
27  }
```

Yes, it is a bit weird to store necklaces, at least in real life. This is just an example, intended to learn how to pick strings entered by the user so let's be imaginative 😊

If you execute it, you will see the steps it performs:
1. Shows the initial balance
2. Asks for the amount to deposit
3. Waits for you to type and press Enter
4. Shows the updated balance

We could have solved this in many other ways. If you fancy, maybe you can think about them and try to decide which is the most useful one.

Appendage: a couple more things you can do with strings

As we said before, a string can be a tool to "talk" to the user. We often decorate them so our apps seem more professional... so here I list a couple tricks you can use to manipulate strings: hints to create more complex messages, or to process the ones the user sends through the keyboard. You can play with this now, or later, when we face the upcoming activities. You'll have several chances throughout this book.

Calculate the leght of a string with String.lenght:
```
public static void main(String args[]) {
    String collar = "A necklace containing 76 pearls";
    int lenght = collar.length();
    System.out.println( "The length is : " + lenght );
}
```

Concatenate Strings
We can link together two or more strings in a message, as we already did, using the sign "+".

We can also use the method String.concat to link literals together:
```
"I live in ".concat("Barcelona");
```

Or linking variables together:
```
String 1 = "I live in ";
String 2 = "Barcelona";
1.concat(2);
```
This is posible because *concat* is a method which accepts as both variables or plain text (between double quotations) as parameters. Or, to say it even better, it accepts both kinds of *arguments.*

Comparing Strings
With the *compareTo* method you can compare two strings (using the variable or the plain text) to check wether they are identical. After doing that, you will obtain the result in an int variable. That variable will have value 0 if they are identical, and any other value if they differ. Just like this:

```
public static void main(String args[]) {
    String 1 = "Good morning.";
    String 2 = "Good morning.";
    int result = 1.compareTo( 2 );
     System.out.println("The result is: " + result);

}
```

If you ever want to compare strings without taking into account whether if they are caps or low cases, you can use the *compareToIgnoreCase* method.

Replacing characters

You can replace a specific character for another to "hide" the things you wrote, just as a key 😊 Just do:

```
public static void main(String args[]) {
    String message = new String("My little secret message");
    System.out.println(message.replace('e', 'r'));
```

And you will end up with a message like this one: "My littlr srcrrt mrssagr").

You can cipher as many characters as you wish, and even decipher later.

You can find more string manipulation tips and methods on the official Java 8 tutorial issued by Oracle:

https://docs.oracle.com/javase/tutorial/java/data/strings.html

3. So many different ways

In the previous chapters we learnt the basics of Java programming: what are methods and classes, what variables are -and how many types are there- and even using operators to play with them.

But the moment we start having ideas we want to make real, all this knowledge seems mingy and insufficient. **The programs we have written so far can only play the same sequence of actions, on and on again...** and there are times when we need them to think a bit more.

Could it be possible for our piggy bank app to ask the user what kind of value is he going to deposit, so the app decides what type of variable is needed? Furthermore, wouldn't it be great if the app was able to alert us if we write enter an incorrect value, and gave us the chance to try again?

Of course, it IS possible! (actually, I still haven't found anything that's impossible to code... just things I don't know how to code).

Control Flow statements

To make our programs able of *making decisions* about how to behave in certain situations, what we do is *preventing* those situations and using what we call decision-making, or control flow statements.

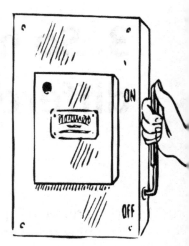

There are 3 types of decision-making statements:
IF   **IF - ELSE**   *SWITCH CASE*

To understand the way these statements work, we can imagine our program like a magical circuit that feeds a light panel. Our circuit is filled with wires: tracks crossed by electricity. Some of those wires have open switches, some others have them closed, and the magic current will only reach the lightbulbs that depend on switches that are "ON".

So, **when the electricity faces a switch, it checks its state to decide if it can go on and feed the lightbulb. If the switch is "OFF" it will skip that lightbulb and go on to the next switch.**

IF - THEN

According to the example from above, we can deduct that the IF sentence is used for making comparisons, to force the program into making questions.

To compose these statements we will also make good use of the operators you already saw on the table in page 34.

For instance, think on our piggy bank app which we already coded. It would be great to add a rule stating that the bank shall only accept positive deposits, it is, deposits that increase the balance. This was the original code:

```
//create a variable to store the amount to deposit
   int deposit = myScanner.nextInt();
       balance = deposit + balance;
```

and we can set up the rule by writing the following:

```
//crete a variable to store the amount to deposit
   int deposit = myScanner.nextInt();
           if (deposit > 0) {
       balance = deposit + balance;
               }
```

Pay attention: With the ">" operator (greater than) we are stating that IF the value of "deposit" is greater than 0, then the code between curly braces can run -and perform the addition. But IF the value of "deposit" is less than 1, then the code between curly braces will be skipped and the app will go on to read the next sentence.

Therefore, this is the proper way of using the IF statement:

```
IF ( elements to compare )  { code block that runs only if the comparison = true ;}
```

We could have used any operator to set up different rules:

- Only admit deposits greater tan 5
- Only admit deposits when balance is less than zero (if balance < 100)
- Only admit deposits if our balance is under 100, AND that limit is not overpassed with the deposit: if (balance<100 && balance+deposit < 100)

Let's perfect our piggy bank!

Adapt your bank app so that it includes the following rules:

- All deposits must be greater than zero
- All deposits must be even numbers

You can re-use the code samples we just saw. What really counts here is that you understand how does this statement work, instead of just memorizing, so it doesn't matter if you need to copy, as long as you understand why is that code correct.

Now you can play with your bank and try to make unadmitted deposits such as wrong concepts or negative numbers.

What happens when you do that?

IF - THEN -ELSE

For now, we have seen that, thanks to the "IF" statement, we can tell our program to perform an operation IF a condition is fulfilled. But, what happens when it isn't? Eventually we may want to go further, and determine that if it's fulfilled the program does "A", and if it isn't then it does "B". Namely, we may anticipate **a code block that is ran only when the condition is NOT fulfilled. That code block is what we call "ELSE".**

This is just like or previous light panel example. With an IF statement you can set a rule such as "if the switch is ON then turn on the light", but **with an IF-ELSE statement we'd be able to set a more complex rule, like "if the switch is ON then turn on the light, and if it isn't, make the alarm go off".** Thus if the light goes on the alarm will remain silent: the code block contained in the ELSE statement can run only when the IF condition is not fulfilled.

Let's look at this Java code example:

```
int freezerTemp = 3;
    if (freezerTemp => 4) {
      System.out.println("Temperature inside freezer too high! "
                      + "It is " + freezerTemp + "C°.")
    } else {
      System.out.println("The freezer is working fine.");
  }
```

This is a piece of code from a hypothetical program that manages an intelligent fridge. This program stores the temperature in an int variable. Then it evaluates if it's over 3 degrees and if that is the case the user is warned. If the temperature value is less than 4 degrees, instead of that warning the user will see a message confirming that the fridge is working as expected. If you try to run this example you'll see that in this particular case the OK message is going to be shown on the screen, and if you change the value of freezerTemp to 4 or greater then the warning message will appear.

The syntax is simple, you just need to **include the new code block right after the IF block:**

Condition
This code block is executed if condition = true

This code block is executed in any other case

46

Ergo:

```
if ( condition ) {
  Action 1;  } else {
  Action 2; }
```

Each block has its own curly braces {} and each action ends with a semicolon;

And there's still more: **you can add as many blocks as you want!** Easy peasy: just **name "else if" all the blocks, from the second one to the penult -and add a condition in each of them**. For instance, here we have a little code that tells us if we have passed our exam -barely passed or with a fantastic grade! - or if we failed it.

```
public class NailOrFail{
      public static void main(String []args){

      int examGrade = 8;

      if (examGrade>=8) {
          System.out.println("Congrats, you nailed the exam.");
      } else if (examGrade>= 5) {
          System.out.println("You passed.");
      } else {
          System.out.println("I am afraid you failed to pass this exam.");
      }

   }
}
```

Pay attention: Although *examGrade*'s value suits the first two conditions (because if it's greater than 8 it MUST also be greater than 4), **once the program evaluates the first condition and finds it is true, it will never enter the second block**; actually, it skips the next blocks of the the IF – ELSE structure. It won't check if there is any other condition fulfilled.

And pay attention to this additional detail: look at how I wrote the conditions. If I were to write "greater than 8", "greater than 5" and "else", if you ever got a 8 or a 5 the program would consider you had failed. Don't you believe me? Then go on, change the value on the variable and try it yourself... 😊

Revamping our piggy bank -again!

Having seen the example from above, you could easily upgrade your bank app again. If you just add and ELSE to the IF you already coded, the program will warn the user if he tries to make and unadmitted deposit, and show him a message explaining that there's been an error and the deposit has been rejected.

Nobody likes that moment when you try to do something, the computer seems unresponsive and totally unable to tell us what's happening, so it is a very good habit to try and foresee errors, so we can go along with the user's actions when something goes wrong.

Did the revamp work? If it wasn't so, on the next page you'll find a possible solution.

Defensive programming!

Defensive programming is a design pattern for our programs. It tries to **ensure that they will work as best as possible, even if the user performs the wrong actions.**
This is extremely useful, not only by making our apps more reliable but because it makes them more difficult to hack.

The principles of this kind of design are a bit too advanced for the point where you are at, but there are a couple concepts you can start bearing in mind whenever you review your own code:
- Write code as **simple** as possible
- Ask your fellow programmers to **review** your code
- **Test** your programs: misuse them, enter the wrong types of data...
- **Re use** that code you already wrote and that works like a charm (like we are doing with the piggy bank).

If you feel like delving into this fascinating topic -right now or in the future- you can check the Wikipedia article for Defensive Programming.

---

solution

Below you will find **a possible solution** for this challenge. There are other things I could have tried, such as moving the sentence

```
System.out.println("Total balance is " + balance);
```

right after line 18, so it will show the balance **only if it has changed**. Remember that, when coding, there are nearly as many ways to write algorithms as little brains can imagine it.

```
1   public class MyPiggyBank{
2       public static void main(String[] args){
3
4           int balance = 0;
5
6           System.out.println("Total balance is " + balance);
7
8           //ask the user
9           System.out.println("Please enter the amount to deposit");
10
11          //new Scanner
12          Scanner myScanner = new Scanner(System.in);
13
14          //create a variable to store the amount to deposit
15          int deposit = myScanner.nextInt();
16
17          if (deposit > 0){
18              balance = balance+deposit;
19          } else {
20              System.out.println("Deposit rejected. You must enter an amount over zero.");
21          }
22
23          //show the updated balance to the user
24          System.out.println("Total balance is " + balance);
25
26      }
27  }
```

The SWITCH statement

Additionally to the IF and IF-ELSE statements, we've got a third tool when we want to control what particular pieces of code are executed: the SWITCH statement.

Speaking literally: a SWITCH is a contact breaker that interrupts the current in a circuit. And that's exactly what the switch sentence does: it **interrupts the path of every instruction that does not comply with the initial condition.** Just like in a pipe network where we can open a stopcock to drive the water through a specific exit, the switch statement is based in a list of possible paths, that the program will travel only if they match the condition.

Let's look at an example to understand how to use this statement.
This is the solution we already used in our piggy bank program, but this time I have replaced the previous if-else statement for a switch structure:

```
//create a variable to store the amount to deposit
int deposit= myScanner.nextInt();

    switch (deposit) {
        case 0:  System.out.println ("Deposit rejected: the amount must be
greater tan 0.");
                break;
        case 1:  balance = balacne + deposit;
                break;
        case 2:  balance = balance+ deposit;
                break;
        case 3:  balance = balance+ deposit;
                  break;
        default:
                break;
    }
    //shows the updated balance on screen
    System.out.println("Your balance is: " + balance);
    }
}
```

Step by step:

- We initiate our switch statement; **we indicate the variable name as parameter** so it will be the base data for the comparison.
- Between curly braces we **list all the cases to compare.** On the example I have listed four cases, foreseeing the deposit value may be 0, 1, 2 o 3.
- Each case contains **an instruction.**

- After each case, the word **"break"** compels the program to exit the switch structure. So when a case is executed, no more cases will be evaluated.
- Additionally you can set a **"default"** case, which means something such as "execute this if the variable's value doesn't meet any of the conditions I have foreseen in the other cases".

It is entirely possible to write a switch block without a default case, or with an empty default case -without instruction inside it. To prove this, you can just comment the default case with the double slash and see how the program still compiles.

Pay attention: We used an int variable for the comparison. The switch statement can also work with chars and even (if you are using Java 7 or later versions) with strings. Always check that the variables you want to compare **belong to the same type**.

As you probably noticed already, this was not the best example of use for a switch statement, because this piece of code asks the user to enter any number. In order to have full coverage of the possibilities, we should have had cases foreseeing any integer number, even negative ones: -4, 0, 5, 658… that would imply writing a huge amount of cases and ending up with complicate and time-consuming code.

So, how do we know what kind of decision-making statement is the right one for each situation?

- If we want to compare **data ranges** (values lesser or greater than) it will often be better to use if or if-else statements.
- If we know for sure that there will only be **a few specific possible values to compare**, a switch statement can be a better choice and produce a cleaner, faster and more legible code.

Armoring the piggy bank

We are going to put this new statement to good use, armoring our piggy bank to face nosey, unauthorized looks ;)
With a switch statement and the Scanner method you already know, we will have our app ask the user for his pass once it starts running. If the password entered is correct the user will be granted and the balance will appear on the screen.
If the user enters an incorrect password, the app will display a message stating that the password is not correct and that this user is not authorized to see the balance.

1. Write the new algorithm, including the instructions to ask for the password, validate it and respond accordingly. It is very important to do this beforehand, so when you start coding you already have a clear design in mind.
2. Try to write the code with this new feature. Remember: this new code block should be placed before the part that manages the deposit. And also, the pass will have to be previously stored, so the program has something to compare to the what the user will enter.

SOLUTION

I'll never get tired of repeating that this is ONE of many possible solutions to the challenge

```
import java.util.Scanner;

public class MyBank {

  public static void main (String []args){
      String password;
      int balance = 0;
      String askForPass = "Enter your password and press Enter";
      String passwordOK= ":::::Welcome to your secured piggy bank.:::";
      String total = " >>> Balance is ";
      String thanks = "::: Thanks for using your secured piggy bank. :::";
      String KO = "Wrong password. You are not allowed to use this piggy bank.";

       Scanner myScanner = new Scanner(System.in); //new Scanner
       System.out.println(askForPass); //ask for the pass
       //create a string variable to store the pass entered by the user
       password = myScanner.next();
       //verify password against the stored one (abracadabra)
       switch (password) {
            case "abracadabra":
            System.out.println(passwordOK + "\n" + total + " " + balance);
            //ask for the deposit value
            System.out.println("Please enter the amount to deposit");
            // create an int variable to store the amount to deposit
            int deposit = myScanner.nextInt();
            if (deposit > 0) {
                  balance = balance + deposit;
            } else {
            System.out.println("Deposit rejected: value must be greater than 0.");
            }
            //show the balance
            System.out.println(total + balance + "\n" + thanks);
            break;
            default:
            System.out.println (KO);
            break;
       }
    }
}
```

A couple details worth looking at:

- We have moved the code that shows the balance, as well as the one that manages the deposit, inside the first case of the switch statement. That part must run only if the switch condition is met, so there was no point in keeping it outside.
- As default case, we have set a message to warn the user if the password is not correct.

Now, for something even more difficult…!

Isn't it a pity that the password appears on the screen when you type it?

Anyone who just wanders behind you while you use your app is able to see it. It's outrageous!

Java provides us with a method called *Console.readPassword* that captures what the user writes (pretty much like Scanner does) without having it shown on the screen.

To call that method you have to import its class, like we did with the Scanner class:
```
import java.io.Console;
```

And then you can delete or comment the line where you stored the text, and write this snippet instead:

```
Console cnsl = null;
cnsl = System.console();
char[] passString = cnsl.readPassword();
String pass = new String(passString );
```

As you can see, its usage is very similar to the way we manage the Scanner method. You have to create a new console object (I called it cnsl), set it to read from the system console, and create a variable (I created the string passString) to store what the user types.
Your app will look soooo professional ;)

4. Child's play

By now we already have some control over our own programs: we can create variables, we know how to manage them with operators, we have used methods to modify them and we can even set different paths for our app according to the conditions it faces.

But our programs still lack for "something more", don't they?

Looking at our piggy bank example, it feels a bit weird when you fail to enter the right pass and it just closes, without a second change of typing it. Sometimes people make mistakes and it's a good thing to have that chance of trying it a second time. But, **how can we ask the computer to perform a specific task a given number of times, without writing the same code block again and again**?

We have some powerful helpers to do that: loops! Like conditional statements in the previous chapter, **loops are tools to control our app's flow of actions**. The difference here is that, **while conditional statements help in deciding what to do, loops help to decide how many times, or for long shall we do it.**

But, what is a loop?

According to the dictionary, a loop is a curving or doubling of a line so as to form a closed or partly open curve within itself. We also use that word for circular airplane maneuvers and for rollercoaster segments where you are twisted and put upside down just like if you had fallen inside a washing machine 😊

So a loop is something that moves in circles around something, so to speak.

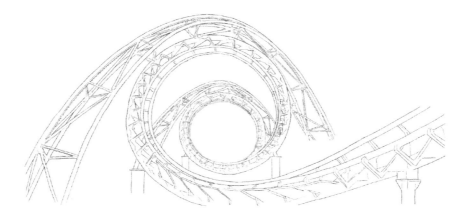

And speaking in programmer's language, when we say "loops" we mean **a code block that is executed repeatedly, until a specific condition is met.**

For the particular scenario of our piggy bank, we can create a loop to give the user more chances to type the right password, asking the app to repeat the sequence *read from the keyboard-compare passwords-deny or grant access* every time the entered key is wrong. And we can even set a maximum number of tries, or allow the user for endless opportunities until he finds out what the password is: the decision is ours.

The Java language provides three types of loops, which we will learn in this chapter:

WHILE - DO WHILE - FOR

WHILE

The while sentence **evaluates the value of a Boolean condition and, as long as it equals true, the code block inside of it is executed**.

1. The program **checks** if the condition is true
2. If it is true, **the code is executed**
3. **Checks the condition again**
4. If it is still true, **keeps on executing the same code**

When -during one of these checks- **the value of that Boolean equals false**, the execution exits the while statement and continues with the rest of the script.

Bear in mind:
- If on step 1 the value of the Boolean is false, the code block contained in the statement **will never get to run**. The condition **won't be checked again** and the loop will be left behind.
- If the condition equals true and it never changes, **we'll be caught in an infinite loop**. *The code block will be executed forever!*

Have you ever heard of tennis ball cannons? Strange question, I know. But tennis players train with ball machines that launch balls on and on, and as long as balls are thrown they keep on hitting them -or at least they try.

That is a good metaphor of a while loop, where the condition would be "are balls being thrown". While the canon shoots, the tennis player will attempt to hit every ball. And when the cannon stops shooting the training exercise will have ended.

That is how we would code a while loop:

```
while(condition) {
  code instructions;
}
```

Just THAT simple!

For instance, this program: a rocket launch simulator:

```
public class RocketLaunch {

    public static void main (String args[]) {
       int countDown = 5;
       String message = "IGNITION";

       while (countDown>0){

         System.out.println(countDown);
           countDown--;
           }
       System.out.println(message);

       }
}
```

Pay attention:

- This time the condition is "if countDown's value is **GREATER THAN** zero". Had we set it as ">=" instead of just greater tan, it would have looped one extra time. **Try it yourself to see why.**
- The sentence countDown--; means **"subtract one from countDown's value"**. As we included thatline inside the loop, that subtract will take place every time the code is executed, that is, after each on screen impression of the variable's value.
- **We show the final message after finishing the countdown** and that is why that line of code is located outside the loop. Had we put it inside then the message "IGNITION" would have appeared after every number. Our rocket would have gone to space by number 5 instead of waiting!

A Little exercise

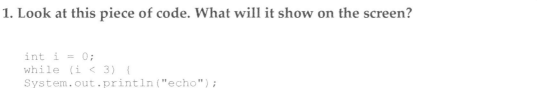

1. Look at this piece of code. What will it show on the screen?

```
int i = 0;
while (i < 3) {
System.out.println("echo");
i++;
}
```

2. There must be something wrong with this code, because I tried to run it and the loop goes on forever... I had to shut the whole thing down! Could you find out what is wrong here?

```
int counter = 0;
while (counter <= 3) {
System.out.println("Message to show");
}
counter++;
```

3. **And yet another one, this is for courageous students:**

Given a specific number (that the user will enter once asked to) **write a program that counts how many times can a number be divided by 2, without residue.** Afterwards the result is shown on the screen.
A possible algorithm would be:

- The program asks the user to enter a number
- The user enters a six
- The program enters a while loop, it divides 6 by 2, and its subsequent result, until it reaches a result that cannot be divisible by 2 (6÷2, then 3÷2 and the result, which is 1,5 cannot be divided without leaving a residue. So the answer is " *2 times*").
- A message with the result is shown on the screen: "6 can be divided by 2 up to 2 times".

SOLUTIONS

1. The word echo will appear 3 times:
echo
echo
echo

2. We caused the infinite loop by leaving the "counter--;" sentence out of the while structure. Therefore, the subtraction won't be performed until the loop is left behind, instead of doing it in every loop cycle. And because the value of the counter will always be the same, the condition to exit the loop will never be fulfilled.

3. I chose to start a loop that functions as long as de result of the division is greater than or equal to 1. Why? Well, plain and simple: there is not a single number under 2 that can be divided by 2 without leaving a residue, so, why keep on dividing once you reach 1?

```
int counter = 0;
 int enteredNumber = Scanner.nextInt();

 while (enteredNumber >= 1) {
   enteredNumber = enteredNumber / 2;
```

```
    counter++;
  }
  System.out.println("It can be divided "+ counter + " times.");
```

There were other ways to do that, as usual. For instance, coding a while statement that keeps on looping as long as *enteredNumber* can be divided by 2 without residue. You can code that condition using the module operator.

DO-WHILE

The Do-While statement is very similar to the plain While, the difference is that, with this one, **first the code block is ran and then the condition is evaluated.**
This means that, whatever the value of the variable is, the code almost runs at least once.

We can compare this sequence to a *piñata* game:

- Hit the piñata with the club
- Check: is the piñata open?
- If the piñata is still intact, hit it again
- Check again, is it intact…?

And so on. Once the variable *intactPinata* equals *false,* we exit the loop and won't hit it again.

As you can see, the operation (hitting the piñata) is always executed once, and then we check whether the condition is true or false. **No matter what its value might be, the code inside the do-while block will always run at least once**. And that's why we call it "DO – WHILE", because it always starts by doing the action.

An easy challenge

Let's go back to our piggy bank app and try to include a do-while statement so, as long as the user keeps entering wrong passwords, the app may keep on asking him for the right one.

Think about it before diving into the code. I strongly suggest you write a draft with pen and paper first, or at least draft the algorithm for the loop.

Some advice for this challenge:
- Remember that the app must ask for the password before the user is allowed to type anything
- The result of the password comparison is the variable to evaluate
- If the user enters the correct key, the loop must finish to let him make his deposit
- If the user enters an incorrect key, a message must appear to warn him about the error and to ask him for the pass again

SOLUTION

```java
import java.util.Scanner;
public class MyPiggyBank{

    public static void main(String []args){
        int balance = 0;
        String pass;

        //new Scanner
        Scanner myScanner = new Scanner(System.in);

        do{
        //ask for the pass
        System.out.println("Please type your password and press Enter");
        //create a variable to store the pass entered by the user
            pass = myScanner.nextLine();
        } while (!"abracadabra".equals(pass)); //stop asking if they are equal

        System.out.println(":::::Welcome to your secured piggy bank.::: \n >>> Your
balance is " + balance);
        //ask for the amount to deposit
        System.out.println("Please enter the amount to deposit");
        //créate a variable to store the amount to deposit
        int deposit = myScanner.nextInt();
        if (deposit > 0) {
        balance = balance+deposit;
                    } else {
        System.out.println("The amount must be greater than 0: deposit rejected");
        }
        //show the updated balance
        System.out.println("Your balance is " + balance + "\n::: Thanks for using
this piggy bank. :::");
    }
}
```

FOR

The FOR statement is a good tool for those situations where we know beforehand **the number of times we need to iterate** (that is, execute the loop).

To code a FOR statement we must first define a variable with an initial numeric value, a second variable with the maximum value to reach; and then we set an instruction so that every time the code block is executed, the first variable grows by one. **The loop ends when the first variable is equal to the maximum.**

Let's imagine this statement as the play-and-seek game. John is going to be the seeker this time, and his six friends are already hiding in the park:

- Variable foundKids that starts with value 0
- Variable hidingKids equals 6
- John starts playing. As foundKids is worth 0, he goes round the park. He finds Maria.
- Now foundKids equals 1. It's still less than hidingKids' value, so he must go round the park again.
- John goes round the park again and this time he finds Mike.
- Now foundKids equals 2, which is still less than the value of hidingKids… therefore he goes at it again.
- If he goes on like this, eventually foundKids will be equal to hidingKids: six and 6. When that time arrives John will exit the loop and stop seeking.

And that, in Java code, looks like the example below:

```
class MyHideAndSeek {
    public static void main(String[] args){
        int hidingKids = 6;
        int foundKids = 0;

        for(foundKids; foundKids<hidingKids; foundKids++){
            System.out.println("1 more turn round the park. John has found " + foundKids
 + " kids so far.");
        }
    }
}
```

Pay attention:

- **The condition in a FOR statement is always constituted by 3 parameters**, in this order: **onset, termination, increment.** That is, the starting value, the value to reach and the increment (or decrement) of the onset variable for each cycle.
- **The FIRST number is always ZERO.** You must always count it, so if you want to loop four times you must set three as limit: zero, one, two and three make four cycles.
- The **onset parameter is always a variable initialized INSIDE the FOR loop.** If you try to initialize it outside the program won't compile, because that variable will be out of the loop's scope.
- The **termination parameter is always an arithmetic comparison**. When it equals false it means the loop's termination.
- The **decrement** parameter is executed **after each iteration** through the loop.
- Notice that I set the termination as "foundKids < hidingKidsMuy" and not as "<="; had I done so, John would have gone an extra round, because the comparison result would not be *false* until foundKids was bigger than hidingKids. And it makes no sense to look for 7 kids when there are just 6. **We must iterate only while John has found LESS THAN 6 kids.**
- Inside the curly braces of the loop we put the code block we want to execute in every iteration, just like we did with the WHILE statement.

Three exercises to practice FOR loops

1. **Write a program that lists all the odd numbers comprised between 0 and 50.**
   Tip: I suggest you check the arithmetic operators table, there is one that serves exactly for this purpose.

2. Write a program that lists all the odd numbers comprised between zero, and any given number entered by the user.

3. Modify the program from exercise 2 so, after listing all the odd numbers, a message appears stating how many odd numbers where found.

   Remember: The message with the total number should appear at the end, after having listed all the numbers.

SOLUTIONS

1. We know what the maximum value is (50) and it's never going to change, so you just need a FOR loop that executes the code fifty times. On each iteration, the code inside the loop will evaluate if the current value of i (which starts at 1) is divisible by 2, or for that matter, an even number.

```
1   import java.util.*;
2   public class OddCounter{
3       public static void main(String[] args){
4
5       for (int i = 1; i < 50; i++){
6           if (i%2 != 0) {
7               System.out.println(i);
8               }
9           }
10      }
11  }
```

2. To code this program, I just added the part where the user is asked to enter a number and modified the FOR loop. Now instead of a specific number as maximum, we have a variable that contains that maximum.

```
1   import java.util.*;
2   public class OddCounter{
3
4       public static void main(String[] args){
5
6       Scanner myScanner = new Scanner(System.in);
7       System.out.println("Please enter an integer number");
8       int num = miScanner.nextInt();
9
10      for (int i = 1; i <= num; i++){
11          if (i%2 != 0) {
12              System.out.println(i);
13              }
14          }
15      }
16  }
```

Pay attention: we set the comparison as "<=". That's because if we just set it as "i < num 2" and the user enters, let's say, a 5, the loop will finish once i is worth 4 and will never check the last number.

Anyway, you must also read carefully what you are asked to do: every odd number comprised in a specific range (including the limits of the range), or every odd number greater than a certain number and lesser tan another.

3. In this exercise I just did the following:
- Created a variable that acts as a counter (for odd numbers)
- Added 1 to that variable every time I found and odd number trough an iteration
- Printed the message after exiting the FOR loop

```
1   import java.util.*;
2   public class OddCounter{
3
4       public static void main(String[] args){
5       int counter=0;
6
7       Scanner myScanner = new Scanner(System.in);
8       System.out.println("Please enter an integer number");
9       int num = miScanner.nextInt();
10
11      for (int i = 1; i <= num; i++){
12          if (i%2 != 0) {
13              System.out.println(i);
14              counter++;
15              }
16          }
17          System.out.println("Between 0 and "+num+" there are "+counter+" odd numbers.");
18      }
19  }
```

Arrays: another way to store data

The Java language provides us with a special structure, designed to **group together a series of variables of the same type.** You can imagine an array as a chest of drawers, storing every variable inside one drawer.

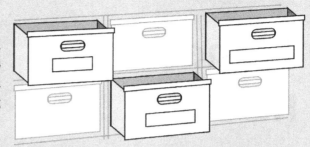

An array of Strings called daysOfTheWeek could be declared like this:

```
String[] daysOfTheWeek = new String[7];
```

This means that I want to initialize an array[] of the string type, called daysOfTheWeek, and that it will contain seven drawers (remember, we always count from zero).

To fill those drawers, you can use this syntax:

```
daysOfTheWeek[0] = "Monday";
daysOfTheWeek[1] = "Tuesday";
```

Where the number acts as index, indicating in what position you want to store the data... and so on. In this example we want to keep the string "Monday" in the drawer number zero.

It is very common to Access arrays using FOR or WHILE statements so we can manage it: we can fill the drawers, empty them, look inside them, comparing their content to some variable... and all of this is done taking the drawer number as reference o index.

In this book, you won't go deeper into this topic, because I considered it will be more useful to use arrays once you learn object oriented programming.

But anyway, it is good to know that they exist. And, if you fancy a little spoiler, maybe in this book's final practice you will have the occasion to work with arrays for the first time ;)

¡OUR FIRST VIDEO GAME!

Game: ROCK, PAPER, SCISSORS

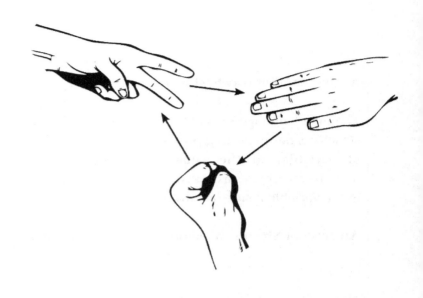

Now that we are seasoned and skilled coders, we are going to gather everything we've learnt, dress it with a couple tricks and create our very first interactive video game.
¡Hooray!

Like good professionals always do, before running at the keyboard we will complete a couple previous phases.

- First we will do some requirement specification. In other words, we'll write down the rules of the game and think about the features our app needs to have. In real life's software lifecycle these requirements are later translated into specific features to code.
- Then we will design the algorithm: the sequence of operations our app will perform
- After that we will -at last!- write the code
- We will test our app to make sure that everything is working as expected
- And then we will re factor: make our code cleaner and more professional to achieve the best results

Let's do it! ;)

Software requirements

This is your first attempt to build a real game and nobody is born wise, so I am going to list the requirements right away. In your following projects I encourage you to do it by yourself, and then try to find out if you missed something important.

These are the features our program must have:

- The program will show a menu after launching
- The start menu will have two options: play and exit
- The opponents will be the user and the machine
- The game will feature the following moves: 1 for rock, 2 for paper, 3 for scissors
- For each round the machine user picks his move using the keyboard, and the machine makes a random move
- Scissor wins paper, rock wins scissor, paper wins rock
- In case of draw the program shows a message to the user: DRAW!
- If one of the opponents wins, a message appears announcing the winner
- The program must foresee the possibility for the user to enter incorrect data on the menus or during the rounds
- In a second version of the game, we could improve it so it keeps on offering new rounds while the user doesn't choose "exit"

THE ALGORITHM

Use your imagination and recreate the whole sequence of a game (from the start menu to the completion of one round). While you picture it, write down every step and express it as a list of events, so you can use them to build your algorithm.

On the next page, you'll find my own algorithm. Try to do it on your own without checking mine before you're done ;)

1. Start menu appears. Options 1) Play 2) Exit

2. If user chooses 2, the application closes
3. If user chooses 1, the game instructions will appear: 1 paper 2 rock 3 scissors. Go to step 5.
4. If the user types any other value, a message such as "incorrect option" will appear and the game will return to step 1
5. The user chooses his move and the new game round starts
6. The machine makes a random move
7. Machine and user moves are compared:
    a. if machineMove == userMove the message "DRAW!" appears
    b. if machineMove > userMove the message "YOU LOSE" appears
    c. if machineMove < userMove the message "YOU WIN" appears
    d. if userMove is not one of the valid values, then the message "INCORRECT MOVE" appears and the game goes back to step 3

Don't you think it was easier than what it seemed? Drafting and designing beforehand helps us face logical problems with better organization.

WRITING THE CODE

To write the code, my advice is to build it feature by feature, verifying after each new development that everything works as expected.

To make it easier, we split the features we must develop. Create a new class and try to follow this steps on your own; after that you may want to check my solution (I will include comments in my code so you understand and see the link between the code and the features).

1. Code the start menu.
Code a menu that will be displayed on the screen and present the options (play or exit) to the user.

2. Code the logic for the menu.
Pick the option entered by the user and, according to his choice: 1) start a round 2) close the app 3) announce the error and repeat step 1
TIP: To exit the app you can use the command System.exit(0).

To control the errors -the user might enter anything different from 1 or 2- I suggest you use some kind of decision making statement.

3. Code the logic for a game round.

Pick the user's input. Make the machine choose a random move.
Compare both moves.
Announce the result: draw – user/machine victory – incorrect input

TIP: The Math class of the Java language includes the *random* method, whose purpose is to choose a random number from a given range. It can be very useful to program the machine's random move.

If you want to use that method you've got to import the Math class first (just as you did with the Scanner class): import java.util.Math).

Here you have an example of this method. This code snippet does something very similar to what you need.

```java
import java.util.Random;
public class random{

 public static void main(String []args){
  //create a new random object
  Random random = new Random();

     /*pick an integer number between 0 and 100, store it inside the
      randomInt variable */

     int randomInt = random.nextInt(100);
        //display the number on the screen
        System.out.println(randomInt);
 }
}
```

And now, I'll let you have a look at how I prepared my new class to start coding. Can you see how I anticipated to the features I needed to implement, creating a skeleton of my program with the comments? This is very helpful when we need to be tidy and focused.

```
1    import java.util*;
2
3   public class RockPaperScissors{
4
5        public static void main(String[] args){
6
7        /*TODO: Code the start menu.
8          This menu displays 2 options (play / exit) on screen*/
9
10
11
12       /*TODO: Code the logic for the menu. Pick the user input and:
13       1) start a round
14       2) close the app
15       3) warn about a wrong input and resume the start menu*/
16
17       /*TODO: the logic for one round of the game.
18       Compare user and machine's move.
19       Announce: DRAW / USER WINS / MACHINE WINS / WRONG MOVE */
20
21       }
22   }
```

SOLUTIONS

As a solution you will find the same class I just proposed, but now with the "TODOs" already
implemented. I have partitioned it in fragments so you can look at the details:

MAIN MENU

```
1    import java.util*;
2
3   public class RockPaperScissors{
4
5        public static void main(String[] args){
6
7        /*TODO: Code the start menu.
8          This menu displays 2 options (play / exit) on screen*/
9        System.out.println("::::::::::::::::::::::::::::::\n"
10                          +"::ROCK, PAPER, SCISSORS::\n"
11                          +"::        WELCOME!       ::\n"
12                          +"::::::::::::::::::::::::::::::\n"
13                          +"Choose an option:\n 1) PLAY  2) EXIT ");
14
```

Notice how I decorated the text so it looks more like a video game should.
Once you get to this point, I recommend checking that the program compiles.

LOGIC OF THE MAIN MENU

```
15      /*TODO: Code the logic for the menu. Pick the user input and:
16      1) start a round
17      2) close the app
18      3) warn about a wrong input and resume the start menu*/
19      Scanner scan = new Scanner(System.in);
20      int option = scan.nextInt();
21      //this loop is in charge of asking the user again if he makes an incorrect input
22      while (option!=1 && option!=2){
23          System.out.println("Please choose one of the valid options:\n"+
24                             " 1 - PLAY  2 - EXIT");
25          option = scan.nextInt();
26      }
27      //once we have a valid option, this switch will manage it
28      switch(option){
29          case 1:
30      /*TODO: the logic for one round of the game.
31      Compare user and machine's move.
32      Announce: DRAW / USER WINS / MACHINE WINS / WRONG MOVE */
33          break;
34          case 2: System.exit(0);
35          break;
36      }
37    }
38  }
```

For the logic of this menu I have used a while statement that is in charge of asking the user as many times as needed, until he provides a valid option.
Once we achieve that valid input we exit the while structure and go on according to what he chose:

- If he chose 1, a game round will start
- If he chose 2, the app will close using System.exit(0);

LOGIC OF A NEW GAME ROUND

This is the logic for ONE round. We still haven't get to the point where we are able to play on and on; as we stated in our requirement list that is something we will approach in following versions of the video game.

And that is why, at the moment, I have put the logic of the round inside of the switch.

```
28      switch(option){
29      /*TODO: the logic for one round of the game.
30      Compare user and machine's move.
31      Announce: DRAW / USER WINS / MACHINE WINS / WRONG MOVE */
32              case 1: Sistem.out.println("Choose your move:\n"+
33                      "0 - PAPER 1 - SCISSORS - 2 - ROCK");
34                      int userMove = scan.nextInt();
35              }
36          //generate a new random move for the machine
37          Random random = new Random();
38          int machineMove = random.nextInt(2);
39          //announce the chosen moves
40          System.out.println("You choose "+ userMove +". I choose "+ machineMove
41                          +"\n::::::::::::::::::::::::::::::::::::::::::::::::::\n");
42          //compare both moves to find the result
43          if(machineMove==0 && userMove==0){
44              System.out.println("DRAW!");
45          } else if (machineMove==0 %% userMove==1){
46              System.out.println("YOU WIN!");
47          } else if (machineMove==0 && userMove==2){
48              System.out.println("YOU LOSE!");
49          } else if (machineMove==1 && userMove==0){
50              System.out.println("YOU LOSE!");
51          } else if (machineMove==1 && userMove==1){
52              System.out.println("DRAW!");
53          } else if (machineMove==1 && userMove==2){
54              System.out.println("YOU WIN!");
55          } else if (machineMove==2 && userMove==0){
56              System.out.println("YOU WIN!");
57          } else if (machineMove==2 && userMove==1){
58              System.out.println("YOU LOSE!");
59          } else if (machineMove==2 && userMove==2){
60              System.out.println("DRAW!");
61          }
62        break;
63
64      case 2: System.exit(0);
65        break;
```

As I have said before, there was not an only way of coding this function. I also programmed it in the most elementary way so you can easily see when is each operation performed and what is the purpose of each statement.

This is an **unpractical approach** -for a coding pro. But with our current skills it is sufficient and stable, hence it's good enough for our goals.

And so the first version of our video game is **ready to start the testing phase!**

LET'S TEST OUR GAME

In the software development lifecycle, there is always a number of operations performed to assess the quality of the product.

These operations consist on trying to detect all the possible scenarios that can take place through the use of the program, and to verify that the app responds accordingly on each of them. Once the scenarios are identified, they are shaped into test cases that will be executed to assess the reliability of the app. If those tests fail the development team will work on the code again to fix the flaws, and eventually the tests will be executed again. The tests are often based on the requirements, the previous experience of the testers and preceding bugs already fixed -because they have a tendency to appear again when we stop looking 😊

I strongly encourage you to execute this tests by playing with your game, so you can detect any errors, defects or unexpected behavior:

- Main menu: choose EXIT
- Main menu: type any incorrect value
- Main menu: choose PLAY
- Round 1: choose scissors
- Round 2: choose paper
- Round 3: choose stone
- Round 4: choose any incorrect value

How did it go? If something didn't turn out ok look at your code again and compare it with my solution until you find what's causing the defect.

LET'S REFACTOR OUR GAME

Refactoring is a process that consists on making changes to our program -without altering its behavior- in order to improve the code.

Namely, refactoring is not about changing what the program does, but improving the code -often by making it simpler- so it makes the app more safe and stable.

Refactoring is a very good habit that helps us keep on learning while enhancing our work.
Is there anything we can improve in our game?

If you look closely, the structure of the game is a bit cumbersome.

We have got a pile of loops, even some nested structures (an IF and a WHILE inside of a SWITCH, more specifically). This makes it complicated to read and what's more important, a little tricky to change, because **when we have so many sentences containing others, making a little change can affect the whole structure**.

The first thing we can do to *clean* our code is enhancing the IF structure. Think about it: we could have saved ourselves three lines by writing "`if(machineMove==userMove)`" instead of doing those clumsy 0 to 0, 1 to 1 and 2 to 2 comparisons. It seems SO evident once you see it...

Besides, we wrote the same strings on and on (to announce draw, victory and defeat) instead of just declaring them as variables at the beginning of the class.

We can make the IF structure look leaner just by implementing these easy changes:

```
//compare both moves to find the result
if(machineMove==userMove){
            System.out.println(draw);
            } else if (machineMove==0 && userMove==1){
            System.out.println(userWins);
            } else if (machineMove==0 && userMove==2){
            System.out.println(machineWins);
            } else if (machineMove==1 && userMove==0){
            System.out.println(machineWins);
            } else if (machineMove==1 && userMove==2){
            System.out.println(userWins);
            } else if (machineMove==2 && userMove==0){
            System.out.println(userWins);
            } else if (machineMove==2 && userMove==1){
            System.out.println(machineWins);
            }
            break;

        case 2: System.exit(0);
            break;
```

And there is still one more benefit: if you ever feel like changing the announcement message, you just need to change it ONCE, in the variable initialization. Being a clean coder really pays off!

And there's still another useful thing we can try.

As you know, many methods are provided by the Java libraries themselves -such as the Random method. Good news is **you can create custom methods too!** You can build them yourself, put them in a separate area of the class and just call them whenever you need them to run.

To create a method with the code that manages a game round, we do the following:

1. Create a new method **outside the main method** (you must never declare a method inside another one). If you have trouble understanding where you should place it, take the curly braces as a guide:

```
public class MyClass{



public static void main(String[]args){



    //space within the main method

  }

    //space within the class, but outside the main method. Here you can
place the "round" method -or any other method you write, for that matter.

}
```

2. **Declare the method**, just like you saw in previous chapters: modifier (private? public?), return type, method name, parameter and curly braces:

```
public static void round(){}
```

3. **Transfer the code** that manages the round, from the "case 1" inside the switch to the inside of this new method. In the space you left in the case you will invoke the method instead of declaring it.
   I strongly recommend you **comment (//) and copy-paste the code from the switch instead of just cutting and pasting it**. Chances are something goes wrong and maybe eventually you'll want to start again, so in case that happens you won't lose the former code, the one that worked correctly.
   Actually that is something you should always do when refactoring: **don't just go and delete things; comment them until you get something that works and then you can erase them safely.** Save yourself a lot of tears.

4. By now the structure of your class looks pretty much like this (and yes, I already deleted my old code, for the sack of good readability of my examples):

```
import java.util.*;

public class RockPaperScissors {

  public static void main (String[]args){

  //main menu
  System.out.println(":::::::::::::::::::::::::::::::\n"
                +":::ROCK, PAPER, SCISSORS:::\n"
                +":::         WELCOME!       :::\n"
                +":::::::::::::::::::::::::::::::\n\n"
          +"Choose an option:\n 1 - PLAY   2 - EXIT ");

          //menu logic
          Scanner scan = new Scanner(System.in);
          int option = scan.nextInt();
          //ask the user again if he makes an incorrect input
          while   (option!= 1 && option != 2) {
          System.out.print("Please choose one of the valid options:\n"+
                    " 1 - PLAY  2 - EXIT");
          option = scan.nextInt();
      }
          //once we have a valid option, this switch will manage it
          switch(option){
              case 1: round();
                break;
              case 2: System.exit(0);
                break;
  }

}
```

Pay attention: after having transferred the code, I place a call to the method instead.
The method we have created doesn't require a parameter, so we leave the parentheses empty - but **really** empty, don't you dare putting a blank space in there!

5. Here you can see the old code, already **inside** the new method. Be careful with deleting or adding extra curly braces ;)

```
...
  case 2: System.exit(0);
  break;
  }


}
   /*Logic for one round of the game.*/
   public static void round(){
   System.out.print("Choose your move:\n"+
                    "0 - PAPER 1 - SCISSORS - 2 - ROCK");

      Scanner round = new Scanner(System.in);
      int userMove = scan.nextInt();

      //this loop controls that the user's move is correct
      while (userMove!=0 && userMove!=1 && userMove!=2){
        System.out.print("Choose your move:\n" + "0- PAPER 1- SCISSORS 2- ROCK n");
        userMove = scan.nextInt();
                                     }
      //generate a new random move for the machine
      Random random = new Random();
      int machineMove = random.nextInt(2);

     //announce the chosen moves
      System.out.println("You choose "+ userMove +". I choose "+ machineMove
                         +"\n::::::::::::::::::::::::::::::::::::::::::::::::::\n");

      String draw = "DRAW!";
      String userWin = "YOU WIN!";
      String machineWin = "YOU LOSE!";

      //compare both moves to find the result
      if(machineMove==userMove){
                   System.out.println(draw);
                   } else if (machineMove==0 && userMove==1){
                   System.out.println(userWins);
                   } else if (machineMove==0 && userMove==2){
                   System.out.println(machineWins);
                   } else if (machineMove==1 && userMove==0){
                   System.out.println(machineWins);
                   } else if (machineMove==1 && userMove==2){
                   System.out.println(userWins);
                   } else if (machineMove==2 && userMove==0){
                   System.out.println(userWins);
                   } else if (machineMove==2 && userMove==1){
                   System.out.println(machineWins);
                   }
      }
}
```

And now the final test: save your changes and see if it compiles. If it doesn't, check my code - and yours- again. You know how to do this, so it's probably just a little detail -such as a semicolon or an extra space here or there.

More fine-tuning

Separating parts of the code that manage specific features -such as the game round code-makes a lot of sense. You can change or upgrade these methods without altering your main method, and even re use them and invoke them as many times as you need.

When we were gathering requirements for our video game we said that in a following version it would be nice to play rounds on and on, without having to restart the app after each one was finished.

Well, that's another benefit of separating code.

We can create a new method, in the same section where we placed the first one (inside the class, out of the main method) and we call it "menu":

```java
public static void menu(){

    Scanner scan = new Scanner(System.in);
    int option = scan.nextInt();

    //this loop is in charge of asking the user again if he makes an incorrect input
    while (option!=1 && option!=2){
                System.out.println("Please choose one of the valid options:\n"+
                                    " 1 - PLAY  2 - EXIT");
                option = scan.nextInt();
    }

    //once we have a valid option, this switch will manage it
    switch(option){
        case 1: round();
            System.out.println("Do you want to play another round? 1- YES 2- NO");
            menu();
            break;

        case 2: System.exit(0);
            break;
    }
}
```

Inside of this method, in "case 1" and right below the call to "round()" we display again the message asking the user if he wants to play another round. And then we call the "menu()" method again.

If you follow the code you will see what this triggers: every time you choose to play, it launches a new game round and then it leads you back to the menu. And that is how we link rounds together, as long as the user keeps on choosing "play".

CHALLENGE ACCOMPLISHED!

5. Follow the trail

All the apps we have coded so far run without leaving a mark in our file system.

In this chapter, though, we will learn how to code programs that are capable of **searching inside our file system, creating new files and saving changes on them**. This will be helpful if, for instance, we want our piggy bank to keep a record of our balance after we shut it down, or if we want our video games to keep track of our winning history.

Some previous concepts about files

Files are not different from the variables we manage in our programs: they are tiny assigned spaces inside our machine's memory, with a specific format and content.

The name that identifies the exact place -inside our filesystem- where the file is located is called the **route.**

For instance, the .class file that contains the video game we coded in our last challenge is called *RockPaperScissors.class*, that is its filename. And, because I stored it in my computer's Desktop, the address (or the *path*) for that file is *C:\Users\Nadia\Desktop\RockPaperScissors.class*.

Try it: Open any folder in your computer (it may be the Downloads folder, the Documents folder... any one will do).
Look at the folder's address bar for the path. Yes, mine is in Spanish!

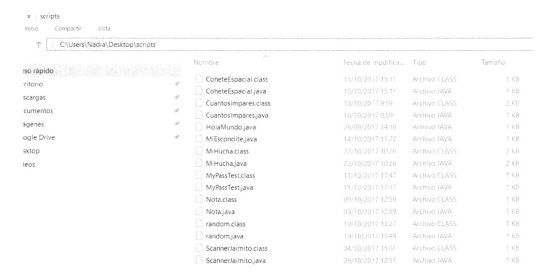

The look of the path may vary from one operative system to another, but the concept is the same.

So now we know that **the *path* is the address that guides us to a file in the computer memory**.

And there are **two possible types of paths**:

Absolute path: Is that one which starts at the root directory of the computer. Therefore the path lists all the folders in the tree, from the root to the file itself.

Relative path: Is the path expressed in reference to the current directory (where you are browsing). So it only lists folders from the spot you are in, to the file itself.

For instance, the path *C:/Users/Nadia/Desktop/Scripts/program.class*, which is an absolute one, could be expressed as */Desktop/Scripts/program.class* if the user is browsing the /Nadia folder, or the program that needs to manage the file is located there, and that would be a relative version of the path: relative to where you already are, so it only lists forward, driving you to the file.

Whenever you write code that manages paths or file locations you'll have to bear in mind what file system are you working with, and whether if you need to use an absolute or a relative path.

The FILE class

"File" is a Java class designed to manage paths -and not files, as easy as it would have been. Even though the name seems to designate the storage item, the class just manages the paths that lead to it.

With the methods that this class provides you can do a lot of interesting and super useful stuff:

- Checking if a file exists
- Creating folders
- Renaming, moving, copying or deleting files (by making the changes to their paths)

Pay attention: The File class' methods cannot read the content of those files; we'll get to do that later.

You can use this class pretty much as you did when working with Scanner and Random (although File is more a datatype tan a collection of methods):

1. Import java.io.File at the beginning of the class, before you declare it
2. Instantiate File with the sentence `File file = new File(String filePath);`
3. As usual, you can name the object as you wish (no need to call it *file)* and inside the parentheses you can put a String variable containing the path (like I did in the second step of this list) or just write the path right away.

To sum up, once File is instantiated I can create a new File object -that will represent a path- using a variable:

Here I create a String to contain the path:
```
String notesPath = "c:/Documents/Homework/Notes/thursdaynotes.doc";
```
Here I instantiate File and create a File object to represent the path I stored inside notesPath
```
File myNotes = (notesPath);
```

Or I can skip the variable creation and just instantiate File like this:
```
File myNotes = ("c:/Documentos/Deberes/Apuntes/apuntesJueves.doc");
```

I prefer working with variables, because it allows for easier maintainability of the code. If the path changes I just need to change the variable once and don't have to go inside the methods. I can also ask the user for the path every time my programs open.

Some useful methods from the file class

Below you have a list of the most useful and simple methods you can use to manage file paths and folders:

.exists() Checks if a given file exists. It's nice to execute this first, as a precaution, before executing methods that work on the files. Hence you can avoid ugly errors if the method that has to read a folder is unable to find it, for example.
This method generates a Boolean variable that equals true or false according to the existence of the given file.

```
File file = new File(path);
bool fileExists = file.exists();
System.out.println("Is the file there?: "+ fileExists);
```

.mkdir() (o mkdirs) Creates a new folder, and generates a Boolean that confirms whether the operation was successful.

```
File file = new File(path);
bool createDir = file.mkdir();
System.out.println("Has the folder been created?: "+ existeArchivo);
```

.renameTo() This method modifies the name of a file or folder. Bear in mind that when we change the path of a file we are indeed moving it from one location to another. We are not changing the name of the folders that contain it, but moving it to that new folder location -as long as it can find that new path. After performing the operation, it creates a Boolean to confirm if the action was successful.

```
File a =  new File("C:/User/Desktop/Maria.jpg");
File b = new File("C:/User/MyPics/Maria.jpg");
bool movesFile = a.renameTo(b);
System.out.println("Did you move the file? "+ movesFile);
```

As you can see in this example, the file was transferred: the file name remains the same and the only thing that changed was the path. It was transferred from the Desktop to a folder called My Pics.

.delete(); This method deletes a given file and creates a Boolean to confirm the success of the operation.

```
File file = new File("C:/Users/Ana/Desktop/test.txt");
boolean delete = file.delete();
System.out.println(delete);
```

Be aware that it won't transfer the file to the recycle bin, it will permanently delete it. So be careful when testing this method.

TRY/CATCH

Before we dive further into file management with Java, there is a technique you need to master, because the Java compiler will oblige its use when we work with documents.

There's a chance you bumped into exceptions when you wrote your first programs. Maybe you encountered errors that arose when something *exceptional or unexpected* happened during its execution, which your app wasn't prepared to handle.

For instance, in the first version of our piggy bank app it lacked any defense in case you tried to enter a string instead of an integer, and if you tried to do that you ended up with something that looked like this:

```
Exception in thread "main" java.util.InputMismatchException
      at java.util.Scanner.throwFor(Unknown Source)
      at java.util.Scanner.next(Unknown Source)
      at java.util.Scanner.nextInt(Unknown Source)
      at java.util.Scanner.nextInt(Unknown Source)
      at MiHucha.main(MiHucha.java:26)
```

And maybe you noticed that this kind of error always came accompanied by your app closing unexpectedly.

Well, that IS an exception, and although we won't delve in this topic during this book (because it's something you better set aside for the future, when you are more experienced with coding) you should know that there are two types of exceptions (checked and unchecked exceptions, we call them) and that the first type are the ones that make the compiler force us to foresee. And this foresight, in terms of Java coding, implies using a Try/Catch structure.

To sum up: **each time you use a method that throws checked exceptions, even if it Works like a charm, you will be obliged to wrap it in a Try/Catch structure.**

What happens inside the app when an exception appears?

Just in case you were wondering…

Sometimes, even if the app compiles, an unexpected event is produced during its execution (such as, for instance, reaching a method without the parameter it requires, or entering a data of an unexpected type).

The method where this exceptional event takes place will then re-act by building a new object that contains information about the error: why did it happen, the state of the system when it happened… that's what we call *throwing an exception.*

This exception is thrown just like a ball, shot from the first method to the next one -hierarchically speaking. Each time this ball bounces over a method, **they check just in case they keep a code block designed to handle that ball** (that exception). If the method doesn't own that kind of code, it passes the ball again to the next method, and so on until it reaches the main method. Once the exception goes there, if there's still no code that can handle it, **the app closes abruptly.** And that is when you see the error in the app's output, on your console: that's the weird text announcing that an exception of a given type reached the main method.

Some exception types have pretty descriptive names that can help us know what happened:

`InputMismatch` the type of the data doesn't match the type expected
`FileNotFound` the file wasn't found in the given location
`NoSuchMethod` when a call looks for an inexistent method

And often you will also be informed of the line where the error popped up:
`at MyPiggyBank.main(MyPiggyBank.java:26)`

The exception handler components are three: Try, Catch and Finally.

This is an example of how we use them:

```
try {

//here we place the code that forces us to use a try/catch structure

} catch (exceptionType exceptionCustomName) {
//here we place the code that manages the exception. It only runs if the error appears

} finally {
//this code is ALWAYS executed, no matter if the exception was thrown or not
}
```

The purpose of this structure is to tell the app **"I want you to TRY something, but in case it doesn't work out please CATCH the exception -instead of throwing it to another method, and FINALLY please do this action".**

The *finally* sentence is not mandatory, so you won't get a compilation error if you don't include it. But it's interesting to rely on it, because it can be used to clean *junk* or to close processes. E.g., if we use the *try* block to open a file and look at its content, it's a good habit to include a *finally* block dedicated to safely close or save that file -no matter if an exception appears or not- before the app closes or goes on to the next operation.

Particularly due to the fact that upon throwing an exception the program will close, it's important to make sure that we allow it to **fail gracefully.**

For the fussy ones: we said that the finally block is always executed. Well, that's not entirely true.
- Was there a System.close(0) command in the try or the exception blocks, it is easy to anticipate the finally would never get to run.
- If an error occurs inside the finally block it will cause an exception instead, and won't run either.

There is always a "but" :)

A little sample of a try/catch/finally structure

For better understanding we are going to see how to use this technique for the particular case of a code we already used: the countdown program.

This example doesn't require a try/catch structure (we didn't include any method capable of throwing checked exceptions) but I picked it anyway because it's clean and easy to read:

```
public class RocketLaunch{

    public static void main (String args[]) {

            int countDown = 5;
            String message = "IGNITION";

       try{
         while (countDown>0){
              System.out.println(countDown);
              countDown--;
           }
          System.out.println(message);

          } catch (Exception e){

              System.out.println("An exception has occured: " + e);

       }

    }
}
```

Pay attention: I have given a name to the exception (I called it *e* because I thought it would be intuitive) and, inside the *catch* block, a set up a message that will include some information about the exception in case it takes place. When that happens, the system won't display an "e", but a message about the error.

There is a lot more to learn in exception managing, but this is enough for our purpose (namely, to make our compiler happy when using certain classes).

We can now go back to the topic of this chapter: files and folders.

The Scanner class (again)

As you already saw on page 36, the Scanner class contains methods designed to read data streams or messages. So far we have used it to process data entered by the user throughout the keyboard -using tools such as the *.nextInt* method.
This class is also capable of **reading data streams from files located in our system**. If we choose the right method, Scanner can manage strings from a text file and manipulate them as we did with any other string.

If we analyze a text document we can see that, inside of it, data are organized in a sequential manner -like queuing-, and when the processor needs to work with these data it usually reaches them in the same order. That is why we talk about data streams, and you can picture those little data elements circulating, one after another, just like if they were coming out of a faucet.

In the following pages, you will see which methods does the Scanner class provide to read streams from text files.

Byte streams and char streams

You know that a char is a type of data, and that it equals to one character (such as a letter or a number). A byte, on the other hand, is a basic unit of information.

Although they might seem similar, truth is they are different, not only in size (a char can get to double the weight of a byte) but in the type of purpose they can serve. We use bytes to store binary data, and chars to store letters, numbers and other characters.

A **byte oriented file** will hence contain binary information, in the form of adjacent bytes.
And a **char oriented file** will, in its turn, contain text strings separated by blank spaces, line jumps and the like. That would be the case of an article written by you in your text editor.

This is a super simple and elementary explanation, with the only goal of helping you decide if the files you are working with are character or byte oriented.

To inform the Scanner class about the specific file we want it to open, we use the File class in the same way we just learnt: indicating the path to our document.

So, just as -to read from the keyboard- we would do this:

```
Scanner keyScan = new Scanner(System.in);
```

To read from a file we will instead do:

```
Scanner fileScan = new Scanner(File path);
```

Look at this carefully: this is just about using Scanner as usual, but passing a path as parameter instead of passing a system keyboard.

And, to tell Scanner we expect it to read the content of the file, we use the same methods we did when Reading from the keyboard: *nextInt()*, *nextLine()* or whichever one we believe will suite the type of data we need to read.

An example

Create a new document in your filesystem, it will contain the following text:

I have read the whole text.

(I suggest you save it as a .txt document)

And now copy the code below. Be careful with the path, it must be the real path from your computer, not mine.

```java
import java.io.File;
import java.util.Scanner;

public class FileReader{

 public static void main(String []args){

     try{
         //set the path
          File path = new File("C:/Users/Desktop/text.txt");
         //open the reader, pass the path as parameter
           Scanner fileScan = new Scanner(path);

    //set it to read the first line, namely, until the first line jump
         String firstLine = fileScan.nextLine();

         //display whatever it reads on the console screen
         System.out.println(firstLine);
         fileScan.close();

     }catch (Exception e){
         System.out.println(e);
     }


   }
}
```

Pay attention: when I finish working with a file I always, always, ALWAYS close it (*fileScan.close()*). This is as vital as brushing your teeth after each meal.

If you copied the code correctly, the content of your file will appear onscreen when you compile and run the code.

Great! Now our apps can read files!

A couple experiments

1. **In the previous code, replace the method *nextLine()* for *Next()*. What happens if you run this new code? Can you explain why?**

2. **Now replace the method *next()* for *nextInt()*, what happens now?**

3. **Lastly, substitute the line** String firstLine = fileScan.nextLine(); **for this code block:**

90

```
for(int i=0; i<4; i++){
String firstLine = fileScan.next();
//show on screen whatever it reads
System.out.println(firstLine);
}
```
Try to put two and two together. Can you make any conclusions?

SOLUTIONS

1. After replacing *NextLine()* for *Next()* it only reads the first word of the line, because that is how this method works: reading the next line or word, implying "all the text until the next blank space".

2. It throws an exception. This happens because the *nextInt()* method expects finding one or more integer numbers separated by blank spaces or line jumps; instead of that it found strings. We had foreseen this exception and controlled it in the *catch* block, so the error is handled and the exception message appears on the screen.

3. This experiment demonstrates how decision-making statements and loops can be used to read specific parts of a document. This opens up endless possibilities, to name a few:
   a. Reading the content of a file only if it contains specific words
   b. Partially reading a document
   c. Reading a document and concurrently processing and manipulating its content
   d. ... and pretty much anything you can imagine

The PrintStream class

Once you learn how to search and read files, the logical continuation is learning to write new content inside them. And to do that we'll make good use of another class, named PrintStream.

Good news is the most important methods of this class will look familiar to you: println() y print().

print() takes a string as parameter and writes right away on the selected file
println() takes a string as parameter, writes it on the file and then adds a line jump

Bear in mind that:

- **If you want blank spaces in your strings**, you'll have to include them yourself. If you don't, every time the method writes something, it would place it right after the last string it finds, and the texts will be adjacent.
- **If you use these methods on a file that already existed**, its content will be overwritten (and its previous content will be forever lost).
- Just as we do after reading from a file, we also must **close the writing stream** when we finish working on it.

An example

We're going to resume working on the previous code sample (where we learnt how to read from our very own text file).

I have improved it now, so first it reads the content from my file, then it writes new content on it and afterwards it reads it again -so we rest assured the editing went as expected.

```
import java.io.File;
import java.util.Scanner;
import java.io.PrintStream;

public class fileReader{
 public static void main(String []args){

try{
 //set the path
 File path = new File("C:/Users/Desktop/text.txt");

 //PART 1: READ
   //call the Scanner
     Scanner fileScan = new Scanner(path);
  //read and display the content
      String firstLine = fileScan.nextLine();
      System.out.println(firstLine);
         fileScan.close();

 //PART 2: WRITE
 //call PrintStream
  PrintStream writer = new PrintStream(path);

 //declare a text to write
  String text = "I managed to write something!";

 //Write the text on the file and close the stream
  writer.print(text);
  writer.close();
```

```
  //PART 3: READ AGAIN
  Scanner reader = new Scanner(path);
  firstLine = reader.nextLine();
  System.out.println(firstLine);
  reader.close();

}catch (Exception e){
  System.out.println(e);
}


}
}
```

This demonstrates what I said above: if we use printing methods on an already existent file, it replaces the whole content for the new one.

Our electronic piggy bank "remembers" …

Our dear piggy bank had a terrible design flaw that prevented us from growing our savings: each time it finished running it "forgot" the deposit we had made and returned to the initial balance.

But now we know how to read and edit files, so it's about time we **replace the balance variable for a** *savings record* **file.**

Hard-coding!

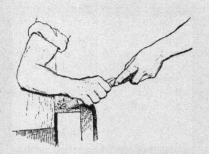

Hard-code, or hardcoding is the name we give to a terrible habit we sometimes see in programmers: it's the practice of **embedding configuration data in the source code**, instead of keeping it externally in a separate file the program can read whenever needed.

This is bad practice, because it forces us changing the source code -which is never harmless, and creates dependency on the coder- every time we need to alter those data. Furthermore, this is the typical detail people forget to update when they translate a program, adapt it to newer versions or expand its features.

Remember: **whatever you hardcode today will be double workload tomorrow**.

Taking the last version of the piggy bank as start, try to perform this alterations in the code:

1. Change the value of *balance* to zero.
2. Produce a *.txt* file that contains a numeric value (it will be the new balance)
3. Implement a method or code fragment that reads from that *.txt* file and stores the content in the *balance* variable. Thus when we display its value, it will actually be the value stated on the file.

1. Implement a method or code snippet that takes the deposit input, adds it up to the balance and writes the result of that addition in the text file. Hence when the user makes a deposit it will indeed be updating the file content.

Don't' forget to wrap that in a Try/Catch structure so it can be compiled :)

Below I copy my previous piggy bank source code, just in case you want to use it as starting point. I think it can be easier to compare our solutions if we are based in the same source code.

```java
import java.util.Scanner;
public class MyPiggyBank {

 public static void main (String []args){
     String pass;
     int balance = 0;
     String requestPass = "Please type your pass and press Enter";
     String passOK = "::::Welcome to your secure piggy bank.::::";
     String total = " >>> Your savings are worth ";
     String thx = "::: Thanks for usin this piggy bank. :::";
     String passKO = "Wrong password. You can't access this piggy bank.";


     Scanner myScanner = new Scanner(System.in); //new Scanner
     System.out.println(requestPass); //requests the pass
     //create a variable to store the user's input
     pass = myScanner.next();
     //check if the pass is OK
     switch (pass) {
             case "abracadabra":
             System.out.println(passOK + "\n" + total + " " + balance);
             //request a deposit
             System.out.println("Please enter the amount to deposit");
             //store that amount in a new variable
             int deposit = myScanner.nextInt();
             if (deposit > 0) {
                     balance = balance+deposit;
             } else {
                     System.out.println("Amount must be greater than 0.");
                     System.out.println("Your deposit has been rejected.");
```

```
                }
            //display the updated balance
            System.out.println(total + " " + balance+ "\n" + thx);
            break;
            default:
            System.out.println (passKO);
            break;
        }
    }
}
```

SOLUTION

Let's divide the solution in a list of steps, so you can read it easily.

1. First I import the classes I will need: *File* and *Printstream* (Scanner was already imported).
   ```
   import java.util.Scanner;
   import java.io.*;
   ```
   Pay attention: That asterisk I put after *.io* helps me import any class contained in that package. So I just put it there and save myself importing both classes separately.

2. Then I change the value of *balance* to 0

3. I initialize the path, right after initializing the class variables:
   ```
   File path = new File("C:/Users/Desktop/scripts/balancerecord.txt");
   ```

4. I Include the try catch so the program compiles:

```
try{
    switch (pass) {

        case "abracadabra":
            Scanner fileReader = new Scanner(path); //new file reader
            balance = fileReader.nextInt();
            System.out.println(passOK + "\n" + total + " " + balance);

        //request the deposit
        System.out.println("Please enter the amount to deposit");

        //store that amount in a new variable
          int deposit = myScanner.nextInt();
          if (deposit > 0) {
             balance = balance+deposit;
          } else {
             System.out.println("Amount must be greater than 0.");
             System.out.println("Your deposit has been rejected.");
          }
```

```
            //display the updated balance
            System.out.println(total + " " + balance + "\n" + thx);
            break;
        default:
            System.out.println (KO);
            break;
    }

}catch(Exception e){

}
```

Pay attention:
- I have placed the **switch statement inside the try/catch**.
- I have declared a new Scanner object (called *fileReader*) specifically to read from the file.
- I have set it up so **balance will adopt whatever value the *fileReader* finds in my file**
- I anticipated a **catch block** but haven't put any code in it yet.

Once I get here, I make sure my program still compiles. Now my first alteration is done: my piggy bank will no longer run based on a hardcoded balance, and will get it from a configuration file instead.

The next goal is to make the piggy bank write on the file. This is how I achieved it:

1. Inside the *IF* statement, right after updating the value of *balance* I create my printstream object passing the path as parameter. I tell it to write the value of *balance* on that file:

```
if (deposit > 0) {
    balance = balance+deposit;

    //call Prinststream
    PrintStream writer = new PrintStream(path);
    writer.print(balance);
    writer.close();
```

2. I have many options for the line that manages the display of the updated balance, but to name a few:
    1. Not altering it, because the value of *balance* is already equal to the one on the file.
    2. Writing an expression that compares the value of *balance* to the value inside the file. If the result is *false* then it can warn the user. I find this option pretty clumsy.
    3. Altering the parameter passed to *System.out.println* so the value displayed ir read from the file and not the variable. By doing that I can check that the addition has been performed, and that the file has been written on.

I chose doing the first, but if you feel adventurous I encourage you to try and code them all, just to experiment and test yourself.

Finally, I polished some details:

1. Inside the *catch* block I include this code so, if an error occurs, it can handle it by warning the user:

```
}catch(Exception e){
      System.out.println(e);
}
```

2. I make sure that all the streams are closed before closing the execution. We had already included a *writer.close* statement but we never got to close the *fileReader*. So I add this line after displaying the balance:

```
fileReader.close();
```

And then I verify that my program keeps on compiling ☺
Now we truly own a real electronic piggy bank that *remembers* our deposits!

FINAL PRACTICE: The Secret File

Congratulations for getting here. Now I want to put something forward: a final practice, **a challenge you can only overcome by using a combination of the skills you acquired with this book.** You'll notice this challenge is more difficult than the previous ones -that's why this is the final practice! -, you can try to conquer it by yourself or use the hints and fragments I will give you.

We are going to build a new game; a super tool intended to **cipher and decipher messages**. We will have the chance to store passwords, secret texts or anything we want to keep safe from unwanted spies… and to even **swap messages with our nearest friends**, if we share our app with them.

How does the text cipher work?

A ciphered text is written with characters that can only be understood by those who know the key, which is the guide to every character's meaning.
There are lots of different ciphers and encryption systems. Actually, Java provides some libraries for this type of developments… but their usage is still a bit advanced for us, so we'll take advantage of this challenge to dive in the past centuries and get to know one of the oldest cipher systems we know.

The Caesar Cipher

Iulius Caesar Augustus was the first of the Ancient Rome's Emperors. He is credited for the Caesar Cipher (or the shift cipher) which, according to history recordings, he utilized to send secret messages to his troops.

This is a rather simple system: it consists on **replacing each letter from the alphabet by another letter, located a specific number of positions down**.

For instance, this would be the replacement pattern for a two-position Caesar Cipher system:

a	b	c	d	e	f	g	h	i	j	k	l	m	n	o	p	q	r	s	t	u	v	w	x	y	z
c	d	e	f	g	h	i	j	k	l	m	n	o	p	q	r	s	t	u	v	w	x	y	z	a	b

Therefore, if we were to write the string "program" using the two-position Caesar Cipher, we should instead type "npmepyk".

Basing on this system we are going to build **a program that ciphers and deciphers messages**. The program will work with a text file located in your computer.

You will be able to distribute this app to some of your friends so you can exchange encrypted messages that only you can turn into readable texts by using the app.

Program requirements

1. **Display a user menu** with two options: cipher and decipher
2. **Read the message from the file and process it** in the desired direction
3. **Save** the new content in the file
4. **Displays the resulting text on screen**
5. Our program is always associated to a **specific file** that already exists

Therefore, to use this program the user must execute it, type his message and request is processing (specifying whether it needs to be ciphered or deciphered).

The Algorithm
Try to write the algorithm for this application. You will find my suggested algorithm below.

Suggested Algorithm

1. The app starts running
2. The app asks the user to enter the message to process
3. The user types the message
4. The app asks the user what to do with the text: 1 Cipher 2 Decipher
5. User chooses 1:
   a. The app ciphers the text
   b. The ciphered text is saved in the preexisting file
6. User chooses 2:
   a. The app deciphers the text
   b. The deciphered text is saved in the preexisting file

Code!

To make it easier for you to organize your work, here you are the image of the main class just as I prepared it to start coding myself:

```
1   public class Encryptum {
2
3     //here I define a dictionary with all the characters allowed in my program
4
5     public static void main(String[] args){
6
7         //an int variable with the positions key
8
9         //ask the user to write the message and store it in a variable
10
11        /*ask the user wether to cipher or decipher the text
12        and save his choice in an int variable */
13
14        /*use a decision-making structure to call the method that
15        does the ciphering/deciphering and writes in the file*/
16
17        //cipher method
18
19        //decipher method
20
21
22     }
23  }
```

I recommend starting off *clean,* and creating specific methods from the beginning to avoid tricky loops and nested structures.

A couple tips:

- **Create a char array as dictionary.** Define it outside the main method so you can access it globally (our cipher and decipher methods will use the dictionary, and they will be located outside the main method too). Don't worry if you don't understand how to work with arrays, I'll supply the methods later.
- **You should define ant int variable that contains the number of positions your cipher is going to shift.** You can store it as a permanent value or ask the user for that number every time the app runs. I pitched upon living it permanent so it will always be 5.

This is the char array I used as dictionary:

```
static char[] chars = {
    'a', 'b', 'c', 'd', 'e', 'f', 'g', 'h',
    'i', 'j', 'k', 'l', 'm', 'n', 'o', 'p',
    'q', 'r', 's', 't', 'u', 'v', 'w', 'x',
    'y', 'z', '0', '1', '2', '3', '4', '5',
    '6', '7', '8', '9', 'A', 'B', 'C', 'D',
    'E', 'F', 'G', 'H', 'I', 'J', 'K', 'L',
    'M', 'N', 'O', 'P', 'Q', 'R', 'S', 'T',
    'U', 'V', 'W', 'X', 'Y', 'Z', '!', '@',
    '#', '$', '%', '^', '&', '(', ')', '+',
    '-', '*', '/', '[', ']', '{', '}', '=',
    '<', '>', '?', '_', '"', '.', ',', ' '
};
```

How to code the dipher and decipher methods

The behavior of these methods is pretty straightforward, but indeed laborious to code:

- **Dump the content of the text input string inside a new char array**
- For every char in the new array, it goes over the dictionary searching for it
- When it finds the coincident char, it shifts the desired number of positions and finds the char that will replace the first one

Try to code it by yourself. It doesn't matter if you don't succeed, it's an interesting exercise that will help you design and test your method.

If you don't dare trying or didn't make it, here you are my own working cipher and decipher methods. You'll still need to make them fit your own code and get it to work altogether 😊

Encrypt:

```java
static String encrypt(String text, int shift)
    {
        char[] readableArray = text.toCharArray();

        for (int i = 0; i < readableArray.length; i++) {
            for (int j = 0; j < chars.length; j++) {
                if (j <= chars.length - shift) {
                    if (readableArray[i] == chars[j]) {
                        readableArray[i] = chars[j + shift];
                        break;
                    }
                }
                else if (readableArray[i] == chars[j]) {
                 readableArray[i] = chars[j - (chars.length - shift + 1)];
                }
            }
        }
        return String.valueOf(readableArray);
    }
```

Decrypt:

```java
static String decrypt(String cipher, int shift)
    {
        char[] cipheredArray = cipher.toCharArray();
        for (int i = 0; i < cipheredArray.length; i++) {
            for (int j = 0; j < chars.length; j++) {
                if (j >= shift && cipheredArray[i] == chars[j]) {
                    cipheredArray[i] = chars[j - shift];
                    break;
                }
                if (cipheredArray[i] == chars[j] && j < shift) {
                    cipheredArray[i] = chars[(chars.length - shift +1) + j];
                    break;
                }
            }
        }
        return String.valueOf(cipheredArray);
    }
```

FINAL RESULT

As a solution, here you are my final source code. Remember: it doesn't matter if yours looks different, as long as it has the same features.

```java
import java.io.File;
import java.util.Scanner;
import java.io.PrintStream;

public class Encryption
{

    static char[] chars = {
        'a', 'b', 'c', 'd', 'e', 'f', 'g', 'h',
        'i', 'j', 'k', 'l', 'm', 'n', 'o', 'p',
        'q', 'r', 's', 't', 'u', 'v', 'w', 'x',
        'y', 'z', '0', '1', '2', '3', '4', '5',
        '6', '7', '8', '9', 'A', 'B', 'C', 'D',
        'E', 'F', 'G', 'H', 'I', 'J', 'K', 'L',
        'M', 'N', 'O', 'P', 'Q', 'R', 'S', 'T',
        'U', 'V', 'W', 'X', 'Y', 'Z', '!', '@',
        '#', '$', '%', '^', '&', '(', ')', '+',
        '-', '*', '/', '[', ']', '{', '}', '=',
        '<', '>', '?', '_', '"', '.', ',', ' '
    };

public static void main(String[] args) {

 //number of positions to shift
 int shift = 5;
 System.out.println("Please type your message and press Enter");
 Scanner reader = new Scanner(System.in);
 String text = reader.nextLine();


 System.out.println("What shall we do?");
 int option = reader.nextInt();


 switch (option) {
  //ENCRYPT
  case 1: //call the encrypter
    String enc = encrypt(text, shift);
    try {
     File f = new File("C:/User/Desktop/scripts/secret.txt");
     PrintStream writer = new PrintStream(f);
     writer.print(enc);
     writer.close();
    } catch (Exception e) {}
    //write the result to the file and display it on screen
    System.out.println("Encrypted text: " + enc);
    break;
```

```
   //DECRYPT
  case 2:
    String dec = decrypt(text, shift);
    System.out.println("Decrypted text: " + dec);
    break;
  }


}

static String encrypt(String text, int shift) {
 char[] readableArray = text.toCharArray();

 for (int i = 0; i < readableArray.length; i++) {
  for (int j = 0; j < chars.length; j++) {
   if (j <= chars.length - shift) {
    if (readableArray[i] == chars[j]) {
     readableArray[i] = chars[j + shift];
     break;
    }
   } else if (readableArray[i] == chars[j]) {
    readableArray[i] = chars[j - (chars.length - shift + 1)];
   }
  }
 }
 return String.valueOf(readableArray);
}

static String decrypt(String cipher, int shift) {
 char[] cipheredArray = cipher.toCharArray();
 for (int i = 0; i < cipheredArray.length; i++) {
  for (int j = 0; j < chars.length; j++) {
   if (j >= shift && cipheredArray[i] == chars[j]) {
    cipheredArray[i] = chars[j - shift];
    break;
   }
   if (cipheredArray[i] == chars[j] && j < shift) {
    cipheredArray[i] = chars[(chars.length - shift + 1) + j];
    break;
   }
  }
 }
 return String.valueOf(cipheredArray);
}
}
```

TEST

It's about time to do some testing on our program.

Design every possible use case scenario and verify what happens when you try it. Some of those use cases could be the following:

- Enter a readable text, encrypt it
- Enter the same text, decrypt it
- Enter a text that contains numbers and caps, try to decrypt it

ENHANCE

Although they might be out of our reach, there are several points that could use a little refactoring and maybe you can engage on that rework in the near future (or now!). Some features that have room for improvements:

- **The number of positions to shift could vary for every execution** (because it is currently hardcode and you unknown that it's a bit clumsy). Furthermore, if the program asks the user for the number of positions, you'll get to share this app with many friends and have a different key for each one of them… so you can exchange messages with a lot of people and they won't be able to cypher other people's texts.

- A latter version of the program **could read from a file instead of the keyboard.** You would be able to send or receive text files and the app would run, load them and process their content. You can even include a feature to list all the files in a folder and let you pick the one to process, or search for it by entering its filename.

- I haven't added any protection in case of user errors -such as choosing "option 3".

6. And now what?

My most sincere congratulations for work-ing your way and getting here.

You have laid a strong foundation so fat, but over all you have demonstrated patience and tenacity.

Programming is something capable of getting the best out of ourselves (perseverance, logic, pon-deration) but also the worst, whenever we can't seem to work things out (frustration, impotence, self-distrust…). **We all get stuck somewhere, sometime** -actually, we do it quite often- and not only during our student years. Professionals make mistakes every day.

If you feel like continuing your Java learning and are wondering what to do next, I can offer you two clues:

1. **Go through your code again:** review what you've learnt and try to include best practices
2. Once you master it, push out into **modular programs and object-oriented programming**.

This book cannot guide you through the second step, as our primary goal was to make you get in contact with the basic Java language structures and datatypes, and help you adopt the algo-rithmic mindset.

But regarding to the first step, I wanted to end this book with a series of good practices or pat-terns that I would like you to consider adopting. They may look a bit abstract here, but I encour-age you to reflect on them while you go through your *old* code again. In due time you will get to see that code has room for improvement – a program is rarely finished and impossible to polish and perfect- and maybe you'll venture into getting back to it and look at it through this new approach. Maybe you'll find a way to make your programs cleaner, simpler and more effi-cient.

There are few satisfactions greater than *beautiful coding.*

DRY (Don't repeat yourself)

Just don't. This is a vital principle that I am sure you can start internalizing. **Try to avoid duplicated code;** whenever you see yourself copying and pasting sentence that will surely mean it's time to extract that code to reusable methods. This rule pursues creating **more stable and maintainable code: it's always easier to make an alteration ONCE** than being forced to alter something tons of times, as many times as it appears on the source code.

YAGNI (You Aren't Gonna Need It)

Can you recall preparing your bag for a holiday trip and stuffing it with a lot of things you never get to use? When we code we tend to do just the same. This principle tells us to **avoid adding features "just in case", because a program with more features is more prone to fails and complicated to maintain.** When designing your apps, include only what you need in that precise moment. There will always be time for updates if you need to add functionality.

The Boy Scout rule

The Boy Scouts have the rule **of always leaving the campground cleaner than they found it.** Apply this motto whenever you refactor or scale an already existing program, especially if it was created by someone else. As we have already said, refactor again and again.

Don't rush to the keyboard

Before you start coding please **write, project, design**. Draw and erase a thousand times what you want to build until you obtain a clear schema. You'll save yourself many hours of method disassembling and algorithm remodeling 😊

Test EVERYTHING

I know it's tempting to take your work for granted once the code compiles, but **your code won't be "done" until you perform the necessary number of tests on it (AND those tests pass).** Even if the compiler doesn't complain, it doesn't mean our program is flawless or behaves as expected when it finally gets to run. Try to list all the possibilities, always. You don't have to just go for *happy paths* or classical, positive use cases, but also for those cases that should fail. And remember that users are unpredictable. There sure are lots of ways of using your app you haven't tough of.

A few people I want to thank...

YOU, for reading this book

Whether you liked it or not, it would make me very happy if you left a review in it **Amazon product page**. Your opinions make me improve my work and help this project go forward.

Remember that you can find **the complete source code for all the practices** in my GitHub repositories: *https://github.com/nadieta*

If you want to subscribe to my mailing list and be updated on upcoming books, you can follow this link:
http://eepurl.com/c9qObn

...

To Saïda and Leila, my *ikigai.*

...

To Albert, for his faith.

Nadia Ameziane Garcia
October2017.